Branch Rickey

THE AMERICAN DIAMOND

A Documentary of the Game of Baseball

with Robert Riger

SIMON AND SCHUSTER · NEW YORK · 1965

ALL PHOTOGRAPHS AND DRAWINGS BY ROBERT RIGER
EXCEPT ENDPAPERS AND PAGE 189, UPI.
DESIGNED BY ROBERT RIGER

LIBRARY OF CONGRESS CATALOG CARD NUMBER: 64-17505
MANUFACTURED IN THE UNITED STATES OF AMERICA
GRAVURE BY PHOTOGRAVURE AND COLOR COMPANY, MOONACHIE, N. J.
LITHOGRAPHY BY COLORGRAPHIC OFFSET COMPANY, NEW YORK
JACKET BY SANDERS PRINTING, NEW YORK
BINDING BY AMERICAN BOOK-STRATFORD PRESS, INC., NEW YORK

CONTENTS

Introduction

Let us talk about

OUR FORMER President Herbert Hoover expressed this tribute to our national pastime: "The rigid voluntary rules of right and wrong, as applied in American sports, are second only to religion in strengthening the morals of the American people . . . and baseball is the greatest of all team sports."

The unique strength in the game of baseball as a team sport lies in the ingenious geometry of the diamond. It is really a game of individuals: nine men and a batsman play out the drama on separate stages as the action unfolds. To be sure, the game has the double play, the hit and run, the squeeze bunt, the relay, but the ten men on the field perform uniquely alone and face their responsibilities alone most of the time. The pitch, the hit, the catch, the throw, the run—again and again. It is almost impossible to find any other team sport that so critically and clearly tests the mettle of each man alone on almost every play and yet fuses them all together into a group working in team competition. That is the paradox of this game that makes it so well suited to the American temperament. Only in baseball can a team player be a pure individualist first and a team player second, within the rules and the spirit of the game.

The greatest single individual contest both in action and in the suspense immediately preceding the action that ever confronts any player in any sport comes when the batsman faces the pitcher. But the game is full of individualistic challenges—a man makes the play or he doesn't. The team is not "hooted" at all when the shortstop makes a grievous error; the unfortunate boy gets *all* the disapproval from everybody. The home run goes down as a personal achievement.

A baseball player's instant response to opposing stimuli is not exceeded even in the sport of boxing. Moral courage, physical skill and empirical ability are all challenged and tested at the moment of delivery of a deceptive pitch, or handling the tag on a ferocious runner, or crashing against the outfield fence.

The field measurements are amazing in producing close plays and decisions. The adaptation of distance to human effort creates exactitudes in timing that control and measure the results of the game. The intermittent rest periods provided by the genius of innings keep the players in repeated preparation for excellent performances. The stolen base makes umpires of a hundred and ninety million. The back-of-the-curtain strategy challenges every managerial mind. The tactics of the game, both elective and superimposed, simple and profound as they are, hold the breathless interest of every spectator. The do-or-die spirit constantly challenges the individual player, not only as a team involvement at the moment, but as an individual expression of prowess and skill. He is on his own.

THE ONLY POSSIBLE POINT of criticism of baseball as our national sport is its lack of participation for old age. Yet in St. Petersburg, Florida, there are two softball teams playing two five-inning games each week throughout the year, whose player membership is limited to those 75 years of age or over. A captain of one of the teams, a pitcher, came to see me in Florida and said, "You qualify. You are past 81. You used to catch. I would like to have you on my team." He was slim and erect and past 94. I told him I would like to catch for him, but unfortunately my contract with the Cardinals prevented me from playing with any other ball club.

Most men my age, if they knew as much about something as I'm supposed to know about this

Baseball

game, would have written ten books by this time. This is my first. I am a complete neophyte—or at least I was when I started, four years ago. It has been one of the most difficult tasks I've ever undertaken. I had good intentions about writing two or three books when I received a book called *The Pros* one day from a stranger. It was on pro football—and magnificent. I spent several days studying this work and realized it was a powerful piece of propaganda on football.

Robert Riger, the creator of *The Pros,* suggested the publisher wanted him to design a sequel on baseball, and he told me that he would do it only if I did it with him. I thought we must do it, but I'm not a writer. He replied, "You're a great speaker. Let's invite them (the readers) over to dinner. You talk to them about baseball and I'll show them some drawings and photographs."

This experience as an author has brought two great pleasures. The first is accomplishing *The American Diamond.* The second is finding a dear young friend in Robert Riger. He believes in all the things he does and does them all with a fierce intensity and pride. Most of all he has a remarkable talent for capturing the significance of an athlete in a single picture or combining several for the drama of a book.

We had healthy arguments late into the night, but it was exciting all the way. Robert said, "When we started this thing you were 81, Mr. Rickey, and I was 35. Now we're finished, and you act like you're 38 and I feel like I'm 84."

This is our book. We dedicate it to the kids from 8 to 38 to 84 . . . and to that 94-year-old pitcher in St. Pete.

BRANCH RICKEY

Branch Rickey

A Young Friendship

I can remember watching so many ball games with him, and the time we drove back to the big white country house set in the rolling hills at Fox Chapel. The trees were young and green and the floor of the woods was covered with a carpet of white portulaca that were pink in the sunset. The house was set under the hill beyond the long barn and the chicken houses, and across the gardens in the back there was a lovely meadow where his son had lived. We came in from the terrace on this beautiful, peaceful May evening and sat down to dinner.

Mr. Rickey quietly said grace as he always does before the evening meal. He carved the meat and filled each plate. There were four of us seated at the table. "George, who do you think was the best third baseman you've ever seen?" Branch Rickey asked the question with the same enthusiasm as a young boy would have asked it. George Sisler was seated to Mr. Rickey's left, and he thought for a moment and smiled and answered in his straightforward way, "Buck Weaver was the greatest third baseman. He could do everything. He would come in to pick up a bunt or a slow roller on the line and his nose would be ten inches off the ground."

When I was a boy growing up over the Polo Grounds, sitting on the rocks of Coogan's Bluff and watching Hubbell beat Ruffing in the rain in the first game of the World Series, or rooting for Dick Bartell and Mel Ott, I never thought I would some day have dinner with Branch Rickey and George Sisler and talk about baseball. But this evening and other evenings are realities now that I will long remember with pleasure. Mrs. Rickey was always at the table and she invariably remembered the players and the teams. When Mr. Rickey and I went out to the workshop office we worked on the manuscript for this book, as we often did, well past midnight.

He was determined from the beginning to write it all himself. With the exception of a few captions for certain pictures, he did exactly that. In fact, he wrote some articles many times over, perfecting them in a manner that he thought would do a person or an idea justice. He rewrote the Ty Cobb piece nine times and refined the very important "Future of the Game" almost as many. "That final piece will get the most attention from baseball people. It has to be right."

A strong-willed man, he loves to plan, plot, manipulate, calculate, think, argue and advise. He always has an open mind, he will reason and accept and tolerate and hope for change and advancement.

Mrs. Rickey was a tremendous force and inspiration in the completion of this book, as were the Rickey daughters, Sue, Jane, Betty, Mary, and Alice, even though the families lived far apart. Mrs. Rickey, watching her husband involved on one occasion in an urgent long-distance phone call, fisting *that* cigar in his mouth, remarked, "He uses that cigar to delay hasty thinking." All his answers were thoughtfully and artfully timed.

He made every day count when we worked together. He loved to laugh and fish and hunt and tell a good story and listen to a good story. He was revered by anyone he ever met, and I believe he never forgot anyone. He was always hopping on a plane and going somewhere to see someone about something. "I've got to talk to him," he would say in his growling whisper, and peer out from under one bushy-white eyebrow. His face was pink and his hair was a dark, gunmetal gray and barely white at the sideburns. His strong, freckled, huge hands with their thick, bent fingers invariably emphasized every point he made in a conversation.

Now that the book is completed, there is a quiet regret because I know I will not be seeing Mr. Rickey or the family as much as before. *The American Diamond* brought us together in a friendship —as all good books bring people together. It is a family book, a boy's book, a book to last for those rare years of adventure and discovery. It is also a book to mark the end of a time. It is a book that will permanently keep the trust between Mr. Rickey, baseball and the boys who love the game.

There is no question that Branch Rickey belongs with the sixteen immortals he chose in the pages of this book. He is one of them. There are only a few hundred Americans in all areas of public life who have lived as significantly as he has in influencing the character of other men. Certainly there are only a few who have contributed to our country's professional sports as his family has— along with the Maras and the Rooneys. They are the blessed families, the ones that had the patience and the courage and the spirit to endure and help bring a game along.

I tried to give a name to Mr. Rickey to describe his unique contribution as a man. He has been called innovator, pioneer, preacher, statesman, horse trader, talent scout, teacher, diplomat, historian. But after seeing him in the long private hours of discussion, and meeting his friends and working with him and knowing him, battling him, loving him, respecting him, I call him *citizen*.

After all—that's what he called Jackie Robinson.
—ROBERT RIGER

PART ONE

The Immortals

How shall we begin? There have been so many books written about the men and the teams of organized baseball that it would seem difficult to be creative and significant in another text. Also, have not all the good baseball pictures already been published? Were not the ones printed in this morning's newspaper very similar to those in yesterday's paper? I wondered too if in one book we could possibly deal with the history of the game and its current decade, when baseball teams and records change so rapidly, and still make the book universal enough to be enjoyed over the years.

In one of our first meetings at the Commodore Hotel in New York Robert and I talked about beginning with a chapter on "The Immortals." "I'm not so sure that one man has the right to call another an immortal," I said. "The word can be abused. We must define it carefully as it refers to baseball." And as we talked it was decided to choose twelve or fourteen or sixteen men who had spent some time in their lives with this great game. There was to be no requirement as to the length of time or the character of the association. The man could be a player or manager or owner or journalist. This was not the criterion. The choice was to be based on what I had learned and seen and heard, in my sixty-five years in baseball, of those men *without whom baseball would not be as it is today*. The immortals were to be those men who *changed* the game or, in any case, left their imprint upon it.

Each in his own special way, the men whom I have chosen truly deserve this distinction, and they become Part I of our book. Robert has done his splendid drawings to complement my writing and to give the reader a picture of the personalities described. Very personal, and yet, I feel, universal.

The sixteen men all have exceptional rights to baseball immortality. They are presented only in a general chronological order. I begin with two old-timers, who gave us the game and the story. There are other choices, I'm certain, and in those nationwide meetings where Americans talk about baseball, other names will be added to the list of immortals. This is only my personal choice, but I am devoted to this group of men—as I am deeply devoted to the game.

BRANCH RICKEY

Alexander Cartwright

LONG AGO there was a young fellow who was fascinated by the possibilities of perfecting a game of ball. In his spare time he would measure various distances on the field near his home and practice throwing to a base against a man running to the base. At night in his room in Manhattan he made many diagrams on paper.

How large shall the playing field be? How shall we design it? How will the game go if the field is this shape or that? How will it go if it is a circle? How will it be if we play the game of baseball on a diamond? What of the players? Will they rotate with one player having a high score? Why not have many players play against each other? How will we place them? What shall be the size of the ball? Its texture? Its resiliency? What about a bat?

Baseball evolved, it is true. It was initially improvised as a hodgepodge fun game without rules, based generally on the British game of rounders. But Alexander Cartwright established its geometry and rules, which made it universal and popular. This American diamond and these rules have remained basically unchanged for over one hundred years.

The legend that Major General Abner Doubleday started baseball is a hoax. The only thing he started was the Civil War, this when he answered the Confederate Beauregard by firing the first shot from Fort Sumter. This legend grew so popular, however, that the National Baseball Museum was erected in Cooperstown, New York, where Doubleday was a schoolboy. A fine soldier and sportsman, he retired to write in 1873. On January 28th, twenty years later, in his obituary in the New York *Times,* there is no reference to baseball whatever.

Cartwright is the man. This New York surveyor is the game's number one immortal.

HE WAS twenty-five years old when he organized the first baseball team, known as the Knickerbockers. After much experimenting on the time and distance factors of hit and thrown balls, Cartwright placed the flat bases 90 feet apart and stationed nine men strategically over the diamond-shaped field to bring the ball and runner to the base a split second apart.

On June 19, 1846, wearing a black swallow-tailed coat with white trousers and a silk top hat, he umpired the first ball game under his rules and specifications, at the Elysian Fields—a resort in Hoboken, New Jersey—between the Knickerbockers and the Excelsiors. That was the first game. His team lost, but he kept the baseball and wrote of using it in a game at Independence, Missouri, in 1849 on the way to the Pacific Coast.

Hearing of the gold strike in California, Cartwright joined 119 pioneers in thirty-two wagons for the westward rush in March, 1849. Reaching his destination, the surveyor remained only a month. He returned by boat, taking a ship that stopped first in China. Cartwright became ill during the voyage and was left off to recuperate in the Sandwich Islands (Hawaii). He recovered and sent for his wife and three children. Before they arrived in 1852, Cartwright had introduced baseball to the islanders. The family remained there until Cartwright's death on July 12, 1892, at the age of seventy-two.

THANKS TO a grandson, Bruce Cartwright, valuable baseball papers and the pioneer's diary were preserved. These Cartwright papers have never been officially recognized as supporting the basic part Cartwright played in the founding and development of the great game.

Cartwright's claim to baseball immortality can easily be substantiated by listing a few of his contributions to the game:

He established baseline measurements.

He created foul-line rules.

He created the foul-strike rule.

He established the team as composed of nine men to a side.

He created the dead ball by limiting the number of bases to be advanced when a ball bounds out of play.

He ruled that a batter can run when the catcher drops the third strike.

He established the rule preventing interference by the runner with a fielding play.

Players, managers, owners, coaches, scouts, writers, commentators, secretaries, ground keepers, maintenance employees, announcers, clerks, statisticians, television and radio employees, ticket salesmen, sponsors—these are the jobs which never would have been, but for Alexander Cartwright.

Today a signpost bears the legend: "Baseball. June 19, 1846: The first match game of baseball was played here between the Knickerbockers and the New Yorks. It is generally conceded that until this time the game was not seriously regarded."

Alexander Cartwright

Organized the first baseball team, established the geometry of the diamond
and the original rules of the game.

7

Henry Chadwick

FOLLOWING CLOSELY BEHIND Cartwright in importance to the game would be Henry Chadwick. Born in England on October 5, 1824, he migrated to this country at the age of thirteen. Young Chadwick, son of an English editor, was the first sports reporter to write of baseball as a specialty in a daily newspaper. The granddaddy of the baseball writers was also guild editor, statistician, and watchdog of the game. This was in 1858, and the following year he edited Beadle's dime-series baseball book. He also devised the game's first box score.

Henry Chadwick

Although Henry Chadwick's major interest was baseball, his talents were many and diversified. He played chess brilliantly and wrote books on the game. He was accomplished at billiards. He was skilled at cricket and wrote of it as an expert. He taught music, played the piano with artistry and composed in the classical vein.

Chadwick's first writing efforts were for the Long Island *Star* when he was twenty. In 1856 he started writing sports for the New York *Times*. He became the New York *Herald*'s first baseball writer in 1862. Later he wrote baseball for various New York newspapers and was long the staff baseball editor for the Brooklyn *Daily Eagle*.

Chadwick became connected with the old National Baseball Association in 1858, when that first professional organization was formed. He remained its guiding spirit and supervised—even initiated—many rule changes and regulations pertaining to the conduct of players on and off the field. He openly fought, with voice and pen, gambling and the threat of dishonesty in council. The National League of Professional Baseball Clubs elected him to honorary membership in 1894 and, in notifying him, wrote:

In conferring this membership, this organization pays the highest tribute in its power to one, who, during a number of years almost as great as is usually allotted to a man to live, has unselfishly devoted his time, talents and energies, by voice and pen, to establish Base Ball as the national game of America. At all times and in all places he has diligently worked for its development and battled for its integrity, its honesty and the purity of its methods.

After editing Beadle's dime-series book, Chadwick took over the editing of De Witt's *Base Ball Guide* from 1869 through 1880, at which point the A. G. Spalding Company engaged him to edit the annual Spalding *Official Baseball Guides*. He remained in that post until his death, at age eighty-four, in 1908, after attending the opening of the National League season at Old Washington Park, Brooklyn. He left a wife, to whom he had been happily married for sixty years, and several children and great-grandchildren.

In denying that he was the "father of baseball," as he did on many occasions, "Father" Chadwick once said, "The game never had a father. All that I or anyone else has done has been to develop what was a field exercise long before we took note of it."

After somewhat intensive investigation of the origin of our game, I have come to believe very firmly that Chadwick has stated the facts. However, I am completely sure that Cartwright made the most material and permanent contribution to the game.

Thus the earliest recordings by pioneer principals themselves were made and left by Alexander Cartwright and Henry Chadwick. The contributions of these two forerunners are specific, unclouded, undisputed, and, unfortunately, almost unacclaimed. It is my personal expression of gratitude to include Alexander Cartwright and Henry Chadwick, first of all, among baseball's immortals. Both men belong in the Hall of Fame, but to date only Cartwright has achieved that distinction.

Honus Wagner

IT IS NOT DIFFICULT to accept several of many definitions of greatness and say that John Honus Wagner was the greatest baseball player of all time. In my opinion, he was.

I first saw him in the old Allegheny Park in Pittsburgh in the fall of 1904. He was discovered by Ed Barrow, the greatest all-round baseball general manager that I ever knew. Here and there over the next fifty years I met him frequently. In 1951, as an officer of the Pittsburgh Club, I came to be very close to the then coach of the Pirate team. He was seventy-seven years of age, reported daily all the way from Carnegie, donned a uniform and sat on the bench during all the games. Seldom did he move from the bench because of physical disability. He did not travel with the club. I visited with him often and came to know him—his early life, his family, his ups and downs, his finances, his acquaintances and friends.

The club pensioned him in 1952, and he was not required to report, although he had the run of the place—office, clubhouse, bench. "You have all the rights and privileges, Honus, as if you owned every share of stock in the Pittsburgh Baseball Club." He showed a most compensating gratitude. It was indeed a hard task to come the twelve miles or more—streetcar transportation—every day. He attended very few games thereafter, but he roamed in for the occasional visit. The club had a prominent part in erecting his honorary monument in the public park just beside the entrance to Forbes Field.

Wagner had no complexities. He left no doubt about any characteristic. He did not have many. His was the simple life, indeed. He knew only baseball. Only one man in my acquaintance was more devoted to baseball or cared less about anything else—Satchel Paige.

Honus played baseball from early boyhood. He and his four brothers, together with Carnegie pick-ups, made a formidable amateur team. He got a rudimentary grade-school education. He could read and write, of course, and did some of the one—almost exclusively baseball—and none of the other.

He lived the game. He slept and ate only to play the game. He came to have all the detailed abilities of all the other great players and almost none of the abilities of any of them in any direction unattached to the game. He could field with Wallace, was as nimble and almost as daring as Cobb, could throw with Birmingham or Furillo, could run with Collins, kept as physically fit as Rogers Hornsby, had the power of Delahanty or

Lajoie, close up to Ruth, had as much "line drive" as DiMaggio, was as abandoned in sliding as Pepper Martin and just as sorry if he hurt anyone, was as kindly in disposition as umpire Tom Connolly, was as modest as Sisler, could pull or push the ball as accurately as Frisch or Billy Herman, and had the superb batting form of Lave Cross but without Cross's overstride. What player had an asset not equaled by Wagner? And what was it? No name has ever been mentioned to compare with Wagner's versatility, his ability to play all positions. A grand fellow named Mike Ryba played all positions equally well, but each one well below the Wagner level.

Honus Wagner

HONUS was bowlegged, terribly so. A really big man, more than 200 pounds. When he ran, he did the split. His crotch seemed only fifteen inches from the ground. When he walked or sauntered, as it were, he placed his feet one ahead of the other in a straight line. When the play was over, he had the relaxed body but not quite the indifferent seeming aimlessness of Jackie Robinson.

I can light up my cigar and close my eyes and think of a hundred different things about him. Did you ever see him resting on one leg, most always only one, never seeking to say anything but ever seeming to invite you to say something?

If you have ever met him face to face, or seen his pictures, you will recall his initial desire to smile, readiness to smile—searching the atmosphere for something to smile at. Did anyone ever have a face which showed less sign of being unhappy? Was he ever really worried?

He had two hobbies, tinkering with his automobile and giving boyish attention to his numerous pets. He owned thirty-five at one time. He cared less about money for its own sake than any player I ever heard of. Waddell was more careless in using money, but Waddell was demanding. He would and did manufacture excuses and fantastic reasons to borrow money or get advances on salary, but for some immediate and misrepresented purpose. No such practice or purpose ever entered Honus' head. Honus never borrowed or needed money quickly, although he seldom had any to speak of.

In all his years, he signed contracts as tendered, with only one exception, and he was forty-two or forty-three when that happened. Mr. Dreyfuss, president and owner of the Pittsburgh Club, was kind and considerate, as was everyone, to Honus Wagner.

He took care of his mother until he was well past forty, marrying only after she was gone. He had few friends, none very close, never lost one, never tried for more. He was almost a recluse. Never gregarious but ever busy, he could keep himself satisfied. Really, he was self-sufficient. He dry smoked, or smoked, always the well-known Pittsburgh stogies. A glass of beer regularly. Never food, drink, or diversion to excess. His speech was completely clean.

He did not care to manage in baseball—resigned after a brief engagement. He wanted no responsibility for anyone or anything but his automobile and his pets.

He loved to play, *really loved* to play—not just the adolescent bent toward sport, but an everlasting mature single-mindedness for baseball. He was wont to say that he knew nothing else.

And the time he went to the World Series in Philadelphia in 1929 without a ticket. He couldn't get into the park. Finally, when recognized, he was rescued and given a box seat.

He was a raconteur with his own alleged reminiscences, unembarrassed by careless memory, and without terminal facilities when wound up. When addressing a group of youngsters, he had a great number of silly stock stories such as the one about the dog who mouthed the ball just as Honus was ready to field it. "I threw the dog to first base and the runner was out. How about that?" And another one that went, "The batter who hit the ball over the center-field fence with the bases loaded and not a man scored." Pause. "It was a girl's game. How about that?" And I have heard him give the same stories to adults in an after-dinner speech, and every story ended with: "How about that?"

No ball player ever lived who had less interests outside a baseball park than Wagner. His record of the last year or the past ten years was of no conscious concern to him. He gave no heed to record making. The game today was all that mattered.

When searching in the pages of the baseball record books, I always like to pause and enjoy reading Wagner's achievements:

Bear in mind that Wagner's record-making stopped in 1917, yet many of his marks remain today. Ten years passed before his record of 2,785 championship games played was equaled and surpassed by Ty Cobb, Eddie Collins, Tris Speaker and Stan Musial. . . . Honus Wagner was the first and only batsman to lead the National League a total of eight years in high percentage, with Hornsby and Musial having seven each. Honus batted .300 or better for seventeen consecutive years. He was a perennial leader in extra-base hits and stolen bases. He stole six bases in the 1909 World Series. He was, beyond doubt, the very best of his era.

He was no pedagogue. Would hardly venture to advise an eighteen-year-old rookie shortstop unless sought out or requested. He did everything exactly right himself, but was never the least bit critical of anyone else—however wrong.

When Wagner scooped up a ground ball on a dusty field, the first fifteen feet in the fast flight of the ball was sometimes a dust cloud. One first baseman with careless exaggeration was wont to say that he simply picked out the biggest object from the cloud and caught it. It was usually the ball.

Wagner is the first choice on the all-time baseball team, to perform anywhere or in Wagner's sure baseball heaven. He could make the team at any position, but most baseball connoisseurs would place him at shortstop. Team captain? Never. It would embarrass him. Besides, he would not care about the ground rules or the responsibility of making any. His life was to hit and run and throw. His only upset, visible to others, was his reaction to a wrong call by the umpire, and it had to be *wrong, very wrong,* for you to find it out from Honus. If you looked very quick, you could see it, but no one ever heard it.

What makes him eligible for immortality in baseball? His record? Yes. His love of the great game of baseball? Yes, indeed. If immortality means at all continuity of existence, Honus Wagner is still playing the game.

Honus Wagner

The immortal shortstop batted better than .300
for seventeen consecutive years.

Charles Comiskey

OVER THE YEARS many baseball players have expressed faith in the game they helped develop by investing in a major-league franchise. Of all these, only Charles Albert Comiskey became sole owner of a big-league club. His Chicago White Sox remained an exclusive family property for sixty years. To me the Comiskey name in baseball always had legendary qualities in both first-base play and team management. By originating "off-the-bag" defense at first, and by winning four straight pennants in the American Association, one of the two majors in the 1880's, he made St. Louis a pioneer baseball city.

He became a reality when I was eleven years old by managing "my" team, the reorganized Reds in Cincinnati, about a hundred miles down the Ohio River from my rural home. I followed him in the early 1890's through a weekly edition of the Cincinnati *Enquirer*. He could do everything—hit and play first and manage. He was a giant in my memory. My pride may be imagined a decade or so later when I learned that he had "drafted" me from Dallas, of the Texas League. We had correspondence in January 1905, and he was gracious in accepting my terms.

I MET my "hero" eight years after that correspondence when I managed the St. Louis Browns. One of my assumed duties was to improve my team by obtaining better ball players.

Since we were both American Leaguers, I thought we might discuss an exchange of player contracts. I hopefully visited Mr. Comiskey at his old park on 35th Street in Chicago. His handshake and greeting were warm. At fifty-five he was strong and robust and he seemed to tower over me. He had sharp but kindly eyes and a large, Romanish nose. In a gravelly voice he directed me to a chair. He began talking and I didn't. He recalled drafting me from Dallas eight years before. Ted Sullivan had recommended me—the same Ted Sullivan that had hired him and helped him so much at Dubuque 34 years before! Why, Sullivan had taken him to St. Louis in 1881 at $125 a month for the new American Association . . . and on and on . . .

I never had a notion during our fifteen-minute visit to mention the name of a single player, either his or mine. I felt that Mr. Comiskey wanted to assure me in unmistakable terms and tones that no young whippersnapper could walk into the offices of the "Old Roman," as he was affectionately called, and cajole him into dealing away any of his playing strength.

Comiskey began his major-league career with the St. Louis Browns. After three seasons in St. Louis, Comiskey, ever the great fielder and batsman, was an established star. He had also shown skill in field direction by taking over the team for owner Chris Von der Ahe, first in an emergency. Then he was appointed regular playing manager in 1885 and won the first of four successive runaway major-league pennants. Comiskey batted

.368 in his third year as player-manager. Following the regular season, he led the Browns against the National League champion, Detroit, in a barnstorming "world series." When Detroit won, ten games to five, the unpredictable Von der Ahe broke up the team by selling five of Comiskey's stars. The player loss was enough to indicate a last-place finish for 1888, but Comiskey then displayed one of the prime requisites of a great manager that made him a trail blazer in baseball—the ability to rebuild a wrecked club and win. Baseball fans witnessed the first instance of a manager rallying a "broken" team of leftovers and kid pitchers to win in spite of themselves. Comiskey not only won his fourth straight; he missed the fifth by finishing only two games behind the winner, Brooklyn.

O F THE several factors that made Comiskey outstanding in the development of baseball in this country, the most important and far-reaching was his part in expanding the game. True, he widened the defensive area of first base by playing away from the bag, becoming the game's first mobile first baseman. But Comiskey contributed more off the field than he did on it, especially in expansion. He was a major factor in the birth and growth of the American Association in 1881. Before that league's demise a decade later, he launched the Brotherhood team of the Players League in Chicago.

In spite of the seven-year-old reserve rule in contracts, some 200 players switched from the two major leagues and played a full schedule. The new third major league survived only the single year, and Comiskey's team finished fourth. Almost all recalcitrants were welcomed back to their former teams. Comiskey returned to St. Louis for the 1891 season. When four of the defunct American Association teams were added to the National to form a twelve-club circuit in 1892, Comiskey accepted an offer from John T. Brush to manage his Cincinnati team, which he had transferred from Indianapolis.

Comiskey pioneered still again in Cincinnati by discovering and nurturing the enthusiasm and zeal of a sports writer, Byron Bancroft Johnson, militant sports critic on the *Commercial-Gazette*. The rise of Ban Johnson to baseball eminence really began with Comiskey. An early acquaintanceship ripened into a camaraderie friendship in that first year at Cincinnati, and it led to the first and only expansion of major-league baseball in America. Comiskey was almost singlehandedly responsible for Johnson becoming president of the Western League in late 1893. A year later,

with still a year to go on his Cincinnati contract, Comiskey resigned and bought the Sioux City, Iowa, franchise in Johnson's Western League and transferred it to St. Paul for the season. The National League learned quickly that a twelve-club league was no go, and, in 1900, it dropped four of its clubs from the unsatisfactory dozen. Comiskey and Johnson promptly made several bold moves by taking over strong cities, including three of the four dropped by the National.

A LWAYS BELIEVING that his native Chicago would support two major teams, Comiskey defied the entrenched Nationals on the north side and transferred his St. Paul franchise to Chicago for 1900. North Siders expressed doubt that fans would ever tolerate the smell of the stockyards near Comiskey's 35th Street ballpark site. Johnson then announced that he would presently change the name of his league to the American League. He demanded recognition from the National as a major league. That was the day!

Comiskey hired Clark Griffith from the Chicago Nationals as pitcher-manager for the 1901 White Sox. Griff, already winner of almost 150 games in the National, turned in twenty-four victories for his first year in the American and was largely responsible for Comiskey's pennant victory that year in Chicago. Five years later, Comiskey's team won another American League pennant. This one I remember well, and not too happily, for it was my first year as a regular with the St. Louis Browns. The 1906 Sox were called the "hitless wonders" for cause. Our pitchers succeeded against them, but their great pitching staff had greater success against us. The hitless wonders went on to win the pennant and meet the Chicago Cubs, winners of a record 116 games in the National League race. Yet the White Sox team won the World Series in six games, springing the surprise of the century. Comiskey's third championship club came eleven years later with what is regarded as one of the all-time great teams, the 1917 White Sox. But it was tarnished in 1919 when eight of its personnel were found to have conspired to lose the World Series to Cincinnati.

To the man who had brought the boys up, such conduct was unthinkable and unbelievable. By the time Comiskey had to believe, it was too late for cooperation. Ban Johnson had produced the facts, and the new baseball commissioner, Judge Landis, took over. It has been said often that the blow caused Comiskey's physical retirement from all future meetings. He rarely attended the games at his modernized park after that.

George Sisler

As the baseball coach at the University of Michigan in February 1912, I had asked for varsity baseball candidates through notice in the Michigan *Daily*. While registering and interviewing applicants in Waterman Gymnasium, I was confronted by a handsome boy of 18 with serious gray-blue eyes. He was well-built, about 5 feet 9 inches tall and weighing about 160 pounds. He wore a blue sweater and a well-used fielder's glove on his right hand. He introduced himself as George Sisler, a pitcher from Akron, Ohio, and an engineering student in the freshman class.

"Oh, a freshman," I said. "Too bad. You can't play this year. This inside work is only for the varsity."

Silent and crestfallen, he reflected deepest disappointment as he turned away. A moment later the team captain, Norman Hill, came up to ask if I knew about "that kid in the blue sweater you were just talking to." Norm then told me about his high-school record and asked that I take another look at the boy before dismissing him. I inquired immediately for a catcher. Lo and behold, young Sisler had his high-school catcher right with him, a boy named Baer, and a good catcher, too.

It was a one-minute workout, all that is needed when coaches meet greatly impressive youngsters. This boy was something in grace and delivery on the very first pitch. The freshman battery was made an exception and stayed out with the varsity during the entire practice period. The "workouts" were unforgettable. George pitched batting practice inside the cage regularly and created no end of varsity embarrassment, although restricted to the use of his fast ball. His left-handed speed and control made him almost unhittable.

He was a major-league pitcher right there!

Sensational as his pitching was, he was truly a sight to see with a bat in his hands. A slender left-hander, unknown to everybody, he was actually a threat to the cage pitchers. Such slashing and driving! Good pitches, bad pitches made no difference. Wham! Boom! Waterman Gymnasium had never known such a drubbing. The whole squad seemed to prefer watching Sisler hit to hitting for themselves with Sisler pitching.

The next four years marked him as the greatest of all college players. His sensational field performance featured practically every game. One of the many must be mentioned as illustrative. There was that day when his Michigan team was playing the University of Georgia in Athens. Time was to be called by agreement so that Michigan could catch a train. It was the final inning and Georgia filled the bases with the score tied and none out. Sisler was called in from center field to relieve the faltering Michigan pitcher. After a few warm-up pitches, George struck out the side on nine pitches without yielding even a foul.

Sisler pitched a total of 152 innings for Michigan, won thirteen victories and lost only one—a five-inning game to Princeton in the rain. He allowed twenty runs and fifty-eight hits and struck out 232 rival batters, slightly over one run and 12.5 strikeouts per nine-inning game. When not pitching, he played the outfield. In 297 times at bat, he made 120 base hits for a college-average of .404. I am not certain of his base-stealing record at Michigan, but I do recall him stealing five in a single game. Upon graduation in June 1915, with an engineering degree, he immediately joined the St. Louis Browns, where I had preceded him, first in an administrative capacity and later as field manager.

The most obvious, initial, and immediate impression on meeting George Sisler is one of modesty almost to a point of shyness, and that impression is lasting. He is modest in the sense that, by nature, he meticulously observes all the proprieties of self-effacement in speech and action. But he has another quality, one sometimes regarded as the antithesis of modesty: ego.

Sisler had enough modesty to justify the wide scope of his popularity. Justifiable ego, however, made him a great player. The term, as applied to George, and most great batsmen, simply means an enduring consciousness of one's own rightness, or belief, an inner knowledge that comes out of one's own practice and experience.

George wrote a book on baseball, and it contains a thorough analysis of batting. In it he is articulate and positive. If anyone chose to dispute a statement in it, Sisler would simply feel a sense of sorrow for the critic.

This type of ego is not an asserted claim of superiority to other people. Not that at all. "This is it," says ego, and whoever says it isn't is wrong, and the antecedent of "it" is whatever he is talking about. The greatest enemy a "batting slump" has

George Sisler

Although he beat Walter Johnson twice *pitching*,
Sisler's hitting was more valuable and he was returned to first base.
In 1920 he batted .420 with 257 hits.

ever known is ego. It keeps a man's confidence in himself unshakable. He may go several games without a hit, but he changes neither stance, stride, sweep of bat nor the grip of it. He does not change his bat or his box position. He changes nothing and does not recognize the word "slump." He has had immunity from that malady for years, for ego, as I am using the word, has helped him firmly never to be subject to continued failure as a batsman. And the next day a Sisler will make four hits off the greatest pitcher of the day, a triple, a double, and two "line-fence" singles.

Sisler had this unassailable ego in both batting and fielding. It is the hallmark of true artistry. Ty Cobb had it in the field of rational daring. Babe Ruth, on his way to the bench after striking out, still nurtured future sorrow for the pitcher. Bill Klem had it in umpiring—"never wrong." McGraw had it in field tactics. Rogers Hornsby, as the greatest right-handed hitter in all history, had it more than anyone I know. He could permit no one to tell him or even suggest how to bat. Supreme confidence, if justly acquired, makes men experts in all fields of baseball. If you disagree with these perfectionists, they will courteously dismiss you, or, having insufficient emotional cushion, will get angry. Ted Williams simply had the spitting tendency of many affronted artists, only he did something about it. He spat!

George Sisler was fortified with the ideal temperament for a baseball player, for his will to win was not a savage, uncontrolled emotion. It stemmed from an orderly, regulated mind always subject to his reflexes and will. His intelligent daring, versatility, contagious spirit in contests, his refusal to condone mistakes which were controllable in advance, his brief yet effective words of instruction, and, above all, his marvelous aptitude made him a nonpareil.

More than any player I ever knew, George was able by example more than words to bring his teammates to a unified and insatiable desire to win. Within a week after he came to the majors in late June 1915, he pitched against Cleveland in St. Louis. He struck out nine and beat the ace right-hander, Guy Morton, 3–1. It was a great day for George when he beat Walter Johnson, his boyhood hero, 1–0—in fact, a second time 2–1. He showed such promise of greatness as a hitter while pitching that he was returned to first base, where he had been tried briefly, and finished his first year with an average of .285. During the next seven years playing first base he surpassed practically all records, both as batsman and fielder. His average assists per game have never been equaled, and his league mark of 140 for a 154-

game season remained for twenty-nine years. That figure came in 1920, the year he set the record 257 base hits for a single season that still stands. He led American League hitters with a mark of .420 in one of the greatest seasons any player ever enjoyed.

In his first eight seasons, 1915 to 1922 inclusive, Sisler was in a class by himself as a symbol of individual achievement. His every move on the ball field reflected the artistry of physical perfection. During those eight years he batted .361 and averaged one stolen base every 3.7 games. He climaxed the period with fifty-one steals in one season. But the cold statistics cannot do justice to the full scope of his baseball life. They cannot, for example, reflect the coordination and artistry of a matchless defensive move that Sisler made at first base in Fenway Park, Boston, shortly after joining the Browns.

With none out and Boston runners on first and third, Burt Shotton, our left fielder, caught a fly ball, conceded the run and made a surprise throw to Sisler, beating the runner returning to first base for a double play. Without an instant of hesitation or lost motion, Sisler whirled and rifled the ball with bullet speed and accuracy to Severeid, our catcher, who tagged the runner trying to score from third base. It was the most amazing triple play I ever saw.

Sisler once fielded a routine grounder deep behind first base. Running forward, he lofted the ball toward the bag to meet the approaching pitcher covering. It was a high toss. Then, realizing that the pitcher wouldn't arrive in time, Sisler raced in, *caught his own throw,* and stepped on the bag to retire the hitter.

And it was a climax, because an insidious eye affliction all but ended his career and made play in 1923 impossible. But Sisler fought back and returned as playing manager of the Browns in 1924 by dint of raw courage and determination. He contributed eight more years of fine major-league play, but those marvelous reflexes and the keen eyesight were not as before.

George and his lovely wife, Kathleen, have left a heritage of a daughter and three sons in baseball. George, Jr., is now an astute front-office official of major-league caliber. Dick's 1950 home run for the Phillies beat me out of one more Brooklyn Dodger pennant. He is now managing the Cincinnati Reds. Young David pitched in both major leagues.

George Sisler's distinguished professional career is detailed in the record books, and he has been justifiably memorialized in the Baseball Hall of Fame at Cooperstown, N.Y., with his lifetime average of .341 duly noted.

Christy Mathewson

CHRISTY MATHEWSON's high contribution to baseball was more than greatness as a pitcher. He was what many men want their sons to be. To millions who never saw him, he personified a rare combination of intelligence and physical achievement. His handsome, open face and quiet way of life, on the field and off, reflected dignity and refinement. Very slight acquaintance revealed courtesy and good sportsmanship; deeper acquaintance, an always kindly, yet rugged and uncompromising competitor.

Mathewson was an authentic American hero for a full generation and beyond, and he is revered today and I believe will be always. Rival cities, while bewailing his pitching mastery, held him in high esteem as a superb athlete. He didn't smoke or drink and he had myriad chances and compensating inducements, as do all prominent players. By never playing baseball on Sunday, he nurtured the belief that he was keeping a promise supposedly made to his mother when she let him sign his first professional contract. This adherence occasioned criticism and embarrassment, but he held his base under fire.

Under dire circumstances he was intelligently unafraid, and one may define the word as he pleases. Yet he was never involved in a controversy. He had the moral strength to avoid it. Because he didn't know the meaning of personal fisticuffs, his physical courage was never subjected to use or test.

I knew Christy Mathewson for most of his baseball lifetime. We were together for several weeks in France during World War I as part of the newly organized Chemical Warfare Service. We slept under the same shelter and, during many hours of conversation, I came to understand and respect his attitude toward Sunday baseball.

From his infancy he had a companion relationship with his mother—no secrets on either side. He enjoyed her views about most everything, and it was not necessary for her to exact a commitment from him to assure herself of his conformity to her religious observances. Matty, as I called him, did not need or require any "promises to his mother" in order to observe Sunday as he did. I do not believe that he ever, even privately, found fault with his "promise," if, indeed, one was ever made. He felt that any nonobservance of her teaching would be interpreted by her as her own failure, that if he did not have such respect and love for her as would hold him free from offense, then no promise was any good.

Matty was born to the Gilbert B. Mathewsons in August 1880, at Factoryville, Pa., northwest of Scranton. Though he played little baseball there as a youngster, in later years the town would close shops and declare a holiday on some of Matty's big days. His career really began at Keystone Academy, where he prepared for college. Success heightened his interest in baseball, and he pitched for semi-pro teams after school.

Matty entered Bucknell University in the fall of 1897. He was scholarly by nature, but his great physique and aptitude made him a prominent football player and then a baseball star. His amateur and college record took him first to the New England League and then to Norfolk in the Virginia League for 1900. By midseason, Matty had won a dozen games and lost only one, whereupon his contract was purchased conditionally by the New York Giants for $1,500. After his third loss, the Giants returned him to Norfolk and canceled the deal. He finished with a record of 21 victories for the full season, and last-place Cincinnati quickly drafted him for $100. The Cincinnati owner, John T. Brush, then traded him to the Giants for the once-great Amos Rusie.

MATTY HAD A RECORD of 21 victories for his first full year, 1901, in the National League. He slumped in 1902, when the Giants were termed in the press "the rankest apology for a major-league team." The Giants went west in July 1902 and won only a few games on the trip. During a series in Cincinnati, news came that John J. McGraw had been hired away from Baltimore of the American League to manage the Giants. The entire complexion of the team changed for the better, and much was added to the pitching career of Christy Mathewson.

After the 1902 season, Matty decided not to resume studies at Bucknell. Instead, he married a Lewisburg, Pennsylvania, girl, Jane Stoughton, whom he had met and courted early in his college days. Then came a friendly association with the John J. McGraws, who had married less than a year before. They occupied a New York apartment together, equally sharing living expenses. They traveled together. McGraw, eight years older, was assertive and positive, yet had great respect for Matty's fine mind and his character and higher education. Matty, only twenty-two, quickly developed a deep respect for McGraw.

THERE HAS never been, I am sure, another such player-manager relationship in baseball. It would be unthinkable today. Mrs. Christy Mathewson told me that "in all his career, Christy was never taken out of a game by McGraw; Christy took himself out." This is almost an unbelievable statement as affecting McGraw, but quite believable of Mathewson. However, McGraw once said: "I never had to tell Christy anything a second time. He made a science of studying hitters. Within a few years he had charted nearly every ball player in the National League. He also worked hard on his control. Knowing the need of reserve in a pinch, he never wasted energy and particularly early in a game. When a hit meant a run, or the game, he was as close to being invincible as any pitcher."

Matty had a similarly high opinion of McGraw and did not hesitate to express it to me. For example, McGraw had set a low-limit rule on all card games at home and on the road. Matty sat in one poker game and somehow the limit was raised little by little until it reached a dollar. When the game was over, one young player had lost considerably in view of his means. Upon learning about it, McGraw fined Matty $500, did not penalize the others, and said:

"You're a star. They look up to you. Besides, you knew better!"

"I never got the money back," Matty told me. "Mac made it stick."

But he added without a trace of rancor how and why McGraw never let friendship, sentiment or feeling of any kind supersede the importance of strict conformity to his rules of discipline. Matty also told me with a knowing smile, "I often thought that Mac had the fine in mind when he sent the next contract to me."

Christy Mathewson knew greatness in his first full year under McGraw when he won thirty games. He won sixty-four in the next two. He became a perfectionist in the art of pitching. Any professional pitcher can produce many different directions of the rotation or spin of the ball. Not many have much selectivity, or any at all, in changing the rapidity of the rotation other than the knuckle ball. Mathewson was a master of both. He could explain that the adjustment or combination of the two features, one or both, with changing velocities, accounts for *all* pitches, and he could throw every pitch in the book. However, he predominantly threw only four.

Matty had the finger manipulation of a latter-day Dizzy Dean or Carl Hubbell. He had the fast ball of the ancient great, Cy Young, or the later Bob Feller—it was close to Walter Johnson's. But above all, he had the artistic know-how of pitching unmatched by anyone before or since. Blessed with an almost photographic memory, Matty put it to practical use. He was skilled in games that required memory, such as checkers, chess, whist, and, later, bridge. He was superbly acquisitive in all directions. He played checkers by number, of course, and could handle multiple competitors blindfolded. My own skill at checkers is "country good." I learned from unsympathetic cracker-barrel experts. Yet, I could never win a game from Matty. He had learned all the openings of most games and had pursued each through many variations. I played many games with him on the public boards in St. Petersburg, Florida, without getting better than a draw.

LOOKING BACK over Matty's greatness, the statistics themselves form a shrine for the baseball fan. His pitching in 1908—391 innings and thirty-seven wins—remains one of the greatest individual efforts of all time. Ironic, of course, was that his eleventh loss, 4–2 to the Cubs, cost the Giants the pennant in a replay of the famous "Merkle" game. But his baseball life contained more than enough triumphs to offset this.

He pitched and won three complete shutouts in the Giants' victory over the Athletics in the 1905 World Series.

He pitched no-hit games in 1901 and 1905.

He set a record of sixteen strikeouts in a single game in 1904, and, in 1903, fanned 267 batters. Both strikeout marks stood for many years.

From June 19 to July 18, 1913, he pitched sixty-eight consecutive innings without issuing a base on balls. In several seasons he averaged fewer than one pass every nine innings and he gave up only forty-four passes in the 618 innings of 1912 and 1913, half a pass every nine-inning game. Only Grover Alexander came close to the mark.

When the matchless arm of Christy Mathewson finally failed, so did McGraw's Giants. From 1903 to 1914, inclusive, the Giants finished first five times, second five times, third once and fourth once. During this period, Matty won 347 games, averaging twenty-nine per season. In 1915 he pitched only 186 innings and won eight games, and the Giants finished last. The team and Matty went down together.

Midway through the next season, McGraw arranged a player deal whereby Matty went to Cincinnati to succeed Ivy Wingo as manager. Within a week he was back at the Polo Grounds to manage his Reds to a victory over the Giants. Matty pitched his last game in Chicago on September 4, 1916, against his old Cub nemesis,

Mordecai "Three Finger" Brown, and won, 10–8.

Returning from France after World War I, Captain Mathewson rejoined the Giants as coach and helped train the 1919 team at Gainesville, Florida. Within a year he suffered an attack of tuberculosis and went to Saranac Lake, New York. It was reported that he had been gassed in a gas chamber during training at Choignes, France. That is not true. I went through the exact training with Matty and was with him immediately afterward. He had no mishap after the final field-training exposure. In fact, Matty took part in an impromptu broad-jump contest and out-leaped everyone in our group who cared to try, and by a comfortable margin. He was then thirty-eight years old.

Matty left Saranac within three years to accept the presidency of the Boston Braves and plunged into hard work. "He never should have left," Mrs. Mathewson told me. "The strain was great and too much." He had to return to Saranac and remained until October 7, 1925, when he died at only forty-five. Uncomplaining to the end, he personified the least publicized of all his great records. In sixteen years of active pitching (4781 innings in 635 games) Christy Mathewson was never put out of a game by an umpire. This might well be the Mathewson message to the youth of America—that you can reach the heights of eminence without interfering with the duties of the umpire.

A N ENTIRE NATION mourned for a departed legend, one of the best-loved athletes of all time. All business in his native Factoryville was suspended. He was buried at Lewisburg, Pennsylvania. Most vivid of the many citations in Matty's memory came from the World Series press headquarters after Washington had beaten Pittsburgh in the first game of the 1925 World Series at Forbes Field. It was written by W. O. McGeehan, then sports editor of the New York *Herald Tribune:*

PITTSBURGH, PA., October 8—While the captains and the kings of Baseball were gathered here last night after the first game of a World Series, there died at Saranac the best loved of all baseball players and the most popular of all American athletes of all times—Christy Mathewson.

If Baseball will hold to the ideals and the example of Christy Mathewson, gentleman, sportsman and soldier, our national game will keep the younger generation clean and courageous and the future of the nation secure.

I wish I could have written that!

Christy Mathewson

Ban Johnson

WHEN I WAS ASKED to choose sixteen immortals for my book, *The American Diamond,* many names passed through my mind. The very first one was Mr. Byron Bancroft Johnson, founder and first president of the American League. For seventeen years, Ban Johnson was the czar of baseball in America. He ruled the game. Charles Comiskey had made him president of the Western League in 1893. Even then, at twenty-nine years of age, Ban Johnson had conceived the idea of a second major league. He became baseball's first successful major-league expansionist.

Professional baseball in 1890 was in the doldrums. Ownership was not too far removed from racketeers. Previously, the Western League had a balanced schedule but not much besides to give it dignity in organization or order in the stands or decency in appearance and action on the field. Umpires almost needed physical protection, and Ban Johnson took care of that. He was a new force on the baseball horizon. He had character and ideals and he loved the game. Greedy owners were just above being counterparts of ward politicians. Not many ladies attended the games. Ban Johnson changed that too. He believed that attendance of women at games guaranteed the dignity of the game and its economic future.

The National League said there weren't enough players for another league, and the press at the time supported that position. Johnson frequently answered, "There are not enough players for the last-place club in the National League either."

This czar of baseball was a dominant personality, domineering indeed in a crowd of clashing partisans. I have been with him in meetings when he reminded me of my grandfather, who on one occasion was visiting my father at our old country home. In midafternoon I had accompanied Grandfather and my father as they went over to view the timber on the twelve acres of the Shelpman tract which had been recently purchased by my father. The question was should the timber be cut and the ground cleared. It was a subject for considerable discussion that evening, and at an hour late for me, a youngster of ten years, Grandfather said to my father, "Frank, we will take a 'belly rest' on this thing and discuss it further tomorrow morning." The next morning at breakfast, Grandfather did discuss the question, referring to the kind of timber, the stage of growth, and the amount and price of the marketable product. I will never forget his final remark.

"Frank," said he, "that's the way I think it is and that's the way it is," and he came down with a bang on the table with his fist. And that's the way it was. The timber stood. That was Ban Johnson as he always was in controversy. He made the decisions. He ruled the roost, but he never stopped to crow over it. When one battle was won, he was immediately high-headed for another.

He was a college baseball player, a debater, a law student, a reporter, a ruggedly opinionated advocate of whatever he believed in. Above all, he was a tireless finder and maker of facts to preface every undertaking. The other fellows' facts were to be questioned or modified or disregarded. He dreamed baseball almost aloud, but his dreams did not require psychiatric mastery to find the cause. He was a supersalesman of ideas—a persuader with economic inducements and a finished organizer in new fields.

HE NEVER intentionally deceived. However, it can be said that he might let an adversary stumble along with less than all the facts. To illustrate: Mr. Johnson was responsible for the illustrious George Sisler coming from the University of Michigan to St. Louis. Pittsburgh had a paper claim to George's services, but Johnson knew the rules better, strange to say, than Mr. Dreyfuss, president of the Pittsburgh Club. George P. Codd, mayor of Detroit, and Judge James Murfin, president of the board of regents of the University, knew the law points and the moral issue involved and vigorously pleaded the university's case for George's free agency. George's eligibility to represent the university in intercollegiate athletics was at stake. The National Commission made up of the presidents of the American and National Leagues and Mr. August Herrmann, president of the Cincinnati club, had to have more than right on its side in order to make a decision. Johnson supplied it. He stood viciously pat on the free agency of the player because of the nonconforming with a deadline date for the promulgation of a contract signed long since by a seventeen-year-old high school boy. George was made a free agent. The Sisler case made a file of over 100,000 words covering a period of eighteen months.

Mr. Johnson had time for the minutest detail as well as for big business, such as bringing the

Ban Johnson

A choice for the first immortal in baseball's history.

Shibes into Philadelphia, financier Charles Somers into Cleveland, Charles Comiskey into Chicago, Robert Lee Hedges into St. Louis, and all the others. And bringing Sisler into the American League was not a very minute detail to Mr. Johnson. The organization of a new league to compete with and excel the old one was a succession of battles. He started with the Western League—then came changes here and there with invasion of National League territory. It took more than planning ability to launch the American League in 1901. Johnson was a very great tactician. He could handle the weapons on the field and he could call the plays. However, he was not given to negotiation on choosing a field

for battle. That kind of strategy never occurred to him. He took conditions as he met them—face to face, as he marched headlong toward his objective. He fought where he met the enemy. If he met him, as he did, in St. Louis, he armed himself with the Milwaukee franchise of the old Western League and pocketed the support of the Cincinnati buggy maker, Mr. R. L. Hedges, and then he said out loud to the National League, "St. Louis is a member of the G-R-E-A-T American League." He signed players from the old Cleveland club and from the St. Louis Cardinals and called the club the Browns. And the battle was on, and the time and place was whenever and wherever he met opposition. In contest he was

21

never taken by surprise—contest is not the right word; battle is the word. He never expected quarter and he never gave any. Victory gained, he was, strange to say but very true, fair and generous in terms of settlement and then instant in pursuit to establish a permanent peace—but largely on his own terms.

He had friendly help in writing the National Agreement of Professional Baseball, but Ban Johnson wrote it. It is still, in effect, the basic written medium of order and control in organized baseball.

No victory was ever sought with the idea of destroying anything helpful to the game. The objective was always the good health of baseball, to make it highly respected by the public and profitable to the owners.

He was a great friend of the players, and continuously, in speeches and private conversations, he set out the extraordinary features of the game, inviting youth to be interested in making it a lifelong career. Ban Johnson would have been very proud of the present commissioner's eulogistic brochure dealing with the professional game. He made the game into what is now an acceptable profession. Very few professions place moral and physical requirements so high or economic and social requirements so low.

Byron Bancroft Johnson would debate, not too conciliatingly, Dr. Alexis Carroll's statement that "in general, athletes are not intelligent." The two would not agree on what constituted intelligence, but Johnson would concede "in general" the great scientist's contention that the habit of logical thinking produced it. Johnson would viciously oppose any adverse comment on any phase of the game from any critic.

He would admit that a game played once a week might offer the emotional thrill of anticipating the next play, but not that it could equal the thrills of the daily game of baseball. Football is indeed a very great game in our country, but the punt is one of the few situations that offer no alternative. The kicker might run with it—he might, but not likely. The spectator is engaged only with the effect of the kick. All other offensive plays are complex. In baseball, the public does not have many alternatives to anticipate. The batter will either bunt or hit, and he can only run in one direction when he does either. It is a simple game but deeply profound. It holds suspense almost continuously, and it holds forth seven days a week for seven months, professionally. It is the recreational refuge for trial and trouble and tribulation and all the other alliterative t's of our time. Johnson was right in his analysis of the game and his constant prophecy about its deserving future.

The job of the offense is to score, and just about 100,000,000 of our people know the alternative means of doing it. The job of defense is to defeat the score, and the tactics of placement and pitch are so well known to the same 100,000,000 that the defensive as well as the offensive game makes grandstand managers out of many spectators and listeners-in. Whatever the great game is, Ban Johnson helped make it so, and it would not be so if he had not been.

JOHNSON was only thirty-three when he wrote his first bulletin to the American League club owners in 1901. His long-range concept of baseball conduct and operation was indelibly reflected in two paragraphs of that bulletin, dated May 8, 1901. It read in part:

The Club Managers are requested to institute such reforms as will shorten the games. In some cities of the American League the games have been long drawn out, and there has been much complaint. The catchers hereafter will play up behind the bat throughout the game. This is a standing order.

CLEAN BALL is the MAIN PLANK in the American League platform, and the clubs must stand by it religiously. There must be no profanity on the ball field. The umpires are agents of the League and must be treated with respect. I will suspend any Manager or player who uses profane or vulgar language to an Umpire, and that suspension will remain in force until such time as the offender can learn to bridle his tongue. Rowdyism and profanity have worked untold injury to base ball. To permit it would blight the future of the American League. This bulletin you will please hand to your Manager so that he may impart its contents to the players.

HE PRESERVED and extended the self-respect of players and management and administrative employees. He removed saloons as the meeting place for baseball conferences. He brought men of high character and ample means into the game as owners. He made it possible for players to be accepted in good hotels. He banned liquor from the stands. He made umpiring a respectable and dignified profession. He unpopularized profanity on the field. He changed personal associates off the field.

He established acceptance of professional baseball in the high echelon of our social structure, believing that it would easily percolate down through the strata of culture, even finally including the lowest as well as the best. He democratized a large segment of American life—making the game the social and economic leveler of *everybody*. Neither money, nor name, nor inheritance, nor dress, nor anything except color had much to do with who sat next to whom. If the player could bunt with rare skill, the conversation was pooled without personal background determining its direction or content. A bank president exchanged views with a bricklayer.

He painted the old parks and built new ones. He was bold in adventure. He was the leading man in my early life who impressed me as having little use for people who could and didn't. At our very first meeting in 1913—an informal one— I was seated opposite him at a convivial table with a dozen present, when following a distant uncomplimentary remark about one of his club managers, he loudly ejaculated "No you don't— no you don't," and pointing jerkingly at the manager, he said, "He's my boy, he's my boy." He had no patience with anybody's views contrary to his own.

He proved the naked fallacy of not enough players. He was the earliest advocate of the now trite truth that goodness in competitive sport is relative; that if a club wins in its class or league, it is a good club, so says the public. If it loses, it is not so good, so says the public. Pittsburgh won the World Series from the great New York Yankee team in 1960. Western Pennsylvania said it was the greatest team ever. The whole country agreed. The same Pittsburgh club, almost to a man, finished sixth the very next year. It was regarded as "no good" throughout the country and most certainly in western Pennsylvania. "Goodness" in professional baseball competition and in public appeal depends simply upon whether or not somebody else is better.

Johnson never lost the right to loyalty, but he signally did lose it. His almost compulsory demotion by the owners from his executive functions as president of the American League killed him. That is a long story. He had given birth to the American League and he nurtured it to a long dominance over the National League, which he almost hated. He never called his league the American League. He always said it, the G-R-E-A-T American League.

He is, almost exclusively, to be credited with the exposure of the Black Sox scandal in Cincinnati in 1919. There never would have been a publicized exposure except for Mr. Johnson's continuous investigation. His probity and his honor gave him no hesitant choice to bring to justice some very great players in his own, the G-R-E-A-T American, league. Following the World Series White Sox scandal of 1919, baseball became panicky. The owners felt that the professional game had lost public confidence. It reached out for a savior and decided to supplant the old National Commission with a new boss, to be called the commissioner of baseball. Unfortunately for himself, Mr. Johnson opposed the election of a commissioner, wishing instead that the civil law should handle the matter and thus substantiate and restore public confidence. He lost Mr. Comiskey's friendship—for the Old Roman, as Comiskey was called, could not bring himself to believe that his "boys could do any wrong." He resented Johnson's investigation, and in the fight that followed, Johnson lost the support of the American League owners—all except Mr. P. D. C. Ball of St. Louis. He gave no consideration to any future results to himself, and after he was retired by the American League, he refused the offer of payment of $320,000 still due on his contract as president of the American League. The making or amassing of money was no part of Ban Johnson's life. He lived for the American League and the game of baseball.

I F HE had been the leader of the proposed Continental League, it would surely be in existence today as a third major league of eight clubs. He would never have accepted the promises of the American and National Leagues in Chicago, August 6, 1959, to absorb the eight owners and cities of the Continental League. I doubt if he would have accepted the invitation to meet with them.

Mr. Johnson was never a compromiser. He prepared for exigency like Napoleon and went down like him. He fought like Grant "along this line" and no other. Almost sad to say, he never tolerated a Henry Clay in his close acquaintanceship. He was blatantly "pooh" with compromise. He had many negotiating battles outside of courts of law, and except for the loss of McGraw to the New York Nationals, he never to my knowledge bore a scar. A federal injunction against Lajoie kept the player out of Philadelphia for a time, but he continued to play for Cleveland in the G-R-E-A-T American League as Mr. Johnson wished. He bore no scar.

He died rejected by his tearful erstwhile friends—an anticlimactic end. He died lonely and alone. His contribution to the game from the beginning, and always, is not closely equaled by any other single person or group of persons. He set the stage for baseball to become our G-R-E-A-T national game.

He is my first choice as a baseball immortal.

John McGraw

THE TRADITIONAL "boy and a baseball," symbolic of the American game, was exemplified by John J. McGraw in his youth. He was born in the village of Truxton, New York, April 7, 1873. In early youth he walked miles for a chance in pick-up games; he was forever throwing a stick or a stone; he wore out countless nickel "rockets"; he would throw a baseball, or a baseball-sized object, at a target on the side of the barn until the sun had set and his arm hung limp. He was small, wiry, and tireless. On Sunday, when he served as an altar boy, a baseball bulged in his back pocket.

Personal tragedy dogged McGraw through most of his life. When he was twelve, his mother and four of her eight children died of diphtheria within a period of a few weeks. His father, an Irish-born railroad worker, took to drink and to beating his baseball-playing son for late dinners or broken windowpanes. He made young John a refugee from the shambles he called home. He hid out with neighbors. Baseball dreams and the precious record-rule books edited by Father Chadwick that he hoarded became a rugged cross to which he clung until death came fifty years later. In that half century, however, he lived several baseball legends as a player, manager, and man.

He took the game abroad. The distinguished sportsmen around the world saw his players and the game America loved. In Havana, Dublin, London, Paris, Berlin, Australia, and the Far East, Tokyo and Hong Kong, John McGraw was baseball's ambassador to the world and the game's most illustrious and talked-about personality.

He held this high station, indeed, fought for it and for the organization he loved, until that rainy Friday afternoon at the Polo Grounds in June of 1932 when a notice was tacked up on the bulletin board in the empty clubhouse stating that John McGraw had resigned and Bill Terry, the first baseman, was to be the player-manager. The headlines that evening were sensational. Lou Gehrig, the great Yankee slugger, had broken a 38-year record by hitting four home runs that afternoon against the Athletics. Gehrig's feat was buried on page 3 behind the startling story of the ending of McGraw's career. The illness that prompted his retirement cut short the pain and boredom of a front-office job and the joy and relaxation away from the tensions of the game. John McGraw died in February 1934.

He never had an Ed Barrow. He never scouted individual players, except in the National League, and those only because he saw them in games from day to day.

Mr. Connie Mack would not let loose of a player until he had a substitute that he thought was as good or better. McGraw would get rid of what he called an "anesthetic" whether or not he had an approved substitute. And he knew an anesthetic ball player—one who puts the manager to sleep not knowing that the team is really weak at that playing position.

I don't recall that McGraw ever had an anesthetic ball player. By the time I found it out, he had gotten rid of him. John never went to sleep. He would take all kinds of chances with new material, but his good judgment made an inadequate player's chance very slim. Seldom did McGraw find himself in such dire circumstances that he was without a substitute. In any event, he had in mind where a good substitute was playing, usually within his own league. He anticipated deterioration, located it, and was never caught by lethargic surprise. He knew a year ahead of the grandstand that player X was disposable. He agreed with Ed Barrow that it was better to make the mistake of getting rid of a good man a year too soon than to make the more grievous mistake of holding on to a bad man a year too long. In the first case, the manager was making a mistake of judgment only because he thought he had an acceptable player as a substitute. In the second case, the manager was first unknowingly satisfied with mediocrity, which in a very real sense is also a judgment error, but more than that, he was guilty of thinking the fellow good enough, and therefore had no substitute whatever available. Belated recognition of a failing player leaves a manager in a state of helpless surprise. He is perhaps shocked that the grandstand and press had put the finger of correct disapproval on the player ahead of himself. That means a year or perhaps several years of delay in rebuilding a given position or department.

IT IS TRUE that getting rid of a grandstand favorite involves the hazard of substitute failure. That, however, would not deter McGraw. He never considered fan opinions in managing his teams. He would have readily agreed that it is almost as managerially bad to let the fans influence the club personnel as it is for a manager to let overindulgence in sentiment delay decision on an old or deteriorating player. Sentiment as a determinative with McGraw would have been his greatest enemy.

No player-management relationship ever existed that equaled for intimacy and closeness the friendship between Mathewson and McGraw, yet this friendship never interfered with the diplomatic disposal of Mathewson's contract to Cincinnati. Managerial sentiment is a weakness that is part of a manager's lack of courage—courage better expressed by a four-letter word. McGraw never lacked that kind of courage.

He was not a producer of talent. He never searched for it in the bushes. He had no time for it. It was not his job. He knew, however, as very few did, the prospective youngster. He was a talent developer unexcelled. To many writers unacquainted with McGraw, it will be surprising to learn that he was a painstaking pedagogue with young players. He was a practitioner of private instruction. Certainly he had very much of Ed Barrow's dual ability, first to estimate the individual player, and second to select out of fifty players nine men as a unit, an individual expression of superiority against all opposing teams. As a "team balancer," as I call it, he was equal to Barrow. Several times he sat across the table from me and would point out the increased strength to me of his proposed trade of players. On one occasion in my Cardinal days, he wrote out my batting order (if his deal were made) and asked the pointed and effective question as he threw the paper across to me, "Don't you believe that that lineup is a stronger club tomorrow than you can put on the field today?" His proposed batting order had his tradable players carefully placed in my lineup.

He would give whatever it took to make his club right now a contending club. He was smart, resourceful, quick, and selfishly but inoffensively sound in all player negotiations.

McGraw knew full well the advantage of having the other club coming to him first on a deal, but he was impatient in contriving to have that happen. He went after what he wanted willy-nilly and placed himself (I sometimes thought) in the position of giving "boot"—money boot—in any player deal. He would admit this disfavoring, self-created circumstance, I am sure, if he were to read this. He would not care about the pre-strategy of negotiations. He was out to get what he wanted, and if he got it the price didn't matter.

If I were to choose a manager for an all-time major-league team about to play another team representing any other part of the world, the manager would be John McGraw.

John McGraw

Ty Cobb

The choice for that *one* player for the *one* game that *had* to be won!

Ty Cobb

TYRUS RAYMOND COBB combined talent and genius as no other player in professional baseball. Many players, some playing presently, could equal and a few could exceed him in native or physical qualities. None had his genius, in large part marked by his uncontrollable urge to excel. His genii removed him from all courtesies of sportsmanship when in strife or contest. In physical struggle he was instantly a competitive paranoiac. In rivalry, on or off the field, his genius was a form of insanity, a do-or-die personal effort to beat someone or something. Cobb would have been the only Greek necessary at Thermopylae.

Ty was seventeen when his father was killed by his mother, who mistook Mr. Cobb for a burglar. I have always believed that this tragic event had much to do with Ty's future attitude toward everything and everybody. He became peculiarly responsible for everything that might happen to him. He was acutely independent and on his own for all future time after this tragic accident.

His first year with the Detroit club—when he was eighteen—added to his buoyant aloneness. His teammates mistreated him savagely. His superior playing ability and his statistical record gave him additional aloofness, resulting in unhappiness for Manager Jennings, for the players, and for Cobb. He found his favorite bats broken from time to time, his gloves misplaced. He was indeed to be forever after a lone-wolf player. Jennings "cut him loose," meaning "play as you please," a pedestalization that increased the breach and tension between Cobb and the other players. Cobb had no friends among them—tried for none anywhere, and he extended that attitude off the field as well.

However, he never reached low for associates or tolerated street acquaintance. He coveted closeness to the "brass" in business and in baseball for strictly personal benefit to himself. What social connections he ever had or sought were above himself—never below. He never slew anyone with words. His part in any heated conversation was a statement of conclusions. If denunciation of his adversary was in order, he selected vituperative words and repeated them. He had no mind for extensive variations of name calling, and the repetitive adjectives got their sustained potency from voice tone or gesture or force itself, which in heat he preferred.

There never were two sides to any argument. If Cobb argued a point with uncontrolled zeal, it was because he knew he was right, and he often was. No player, not even Ruth, was more a law to

himself on the field. Cobb lived off the field as though he wished to live forever. He lived on the field as though it was his last day. No player ever practiced turning a base as he did. With real driving speed, he would approach a base bag, trying to touch it with his left foot on hard impact in order to make the turn, as nearly as possible, on a ninety-degree angle. No one ever saw Cobb circle any base. Old players can recall the body twist and strong swing of Cobb in turning bases on his extra-base blows. There have been players who could run the hundred yards faster than Cobb, but surely there has never been one who could run the 120 diamond yards with Cobb.

COBB told me that many base runners in sliding would touch an imaginary bag ninety-three feet from their starting point as soon as they actually touched the ninety-foot bag, the objective of the steal. My observation for many years, supported by pictures, sustains his statement. The base runner, hooking the bag with the left foot on a fall-away slide to the right, will pass the ninety-foot mark with his right foot usually by as much as four feet and seldom by less than two. Their running placement for the slide and their body position on the take off, one or the other or both, are wrong. Infielder Wills of the Los Angeles Club is a Cobb slider. I believe Willie Mays is, too.

Sliding was an art with Cobb. He practiced sliding by the hour in his early years—to the right, to the left, straight and up, ready to run if the ball was bobbled. He practiced missing the bag entirely when apparently clearly out in order to elude the tag and then hand-touch the bag from the rear. Cobb could slide and resume his running without appreciable loss of time. He was a perfectionist by election, by choice that is, and particularly by practice.

I never knew of any player other than Cobb practicing sliding with the intent of using the loose foot to kick the ball out of the baseman's hand. He actually practiced that movement. And Cobb could and did concentrate on it with great effect. It led to the general charge throughout the American League that, on occasion, he intentionally spiked the tagger. I don't think he ever spiked anyone intentionally. But he *has* stated to me that he made two such attempts, which he described in detail—both deliberately in hot revenge. But he was not a cruel player—not in my judgment. He had more bruises from day to day and more permanent scars from spikes than most opponents. As I have said, he carried in his uniform no treatise on the ethics of play, yet in the days of only one umpire, I doubt if he ever cut short of second in running from first to third. Cobb on base anywhere immediately got and held pitcher attention more than the batsman. The great unrealized and almost never-mentioned contribution of Cobb to the winning of games was his constant wrecking of pitcher concentration on the pitch. With Cobb on first, or any base for that matter, many pitchers over a period of, say, twenty years became simply "throwers."

He practiced almost by the clock in throwing from the outfield. His objective was to have the ball skip when it hit the ground on its first contact—not bounce with retarded speed. That meant definite control of the spin and the proper trajectory. Did anyone ever hear of a baseball player who voluntarily and alone would impose upon himself arduous practice of this sort? I never did.

Cobb did not have a great arm, but accuracy and elevation of the throw and right rotation on the ball were his habitual possessions. He never took a double step on his throw from the outfield. He threw now—right now—when he caught the ball. He would say, "The runner is moving at full speed and will run fifteen feet while I am stepping five feet." He was precisely scientific in every physical move. No one ever heard of base runners taking chances on Cobb's arm. No one.

To push or pull the ball as a batsman by advance intent is seldom attempted by even the greatest hitters of the present day. However, it is quite frequent to hear some broadcaster attribute that intent and ability to boys whose chief and only challenge and concern is to get the bat and ball together solidly in *any* direction. More batters are concerned with not striking out than with place hitting.

Cobb mastered the art of hitting to the opposite field with greater effect than anyone I ever knew. His method was simple and, I presume, original with him. He maintained, and of course correctly, that every batsman naturally moves the front foot in addressing himself to the pitch. To hit to the opposite field, Cobb simply firmly held the front-foot position and moved the rear foot (in reality usually stepping back with it), and this changed the timing so that the stroke in effect tended to change the ball's direction—in Cobb's case (a left-hand hitter) from right field to left field. Cobb was my teacher in this technique, and I have passed it on to several one-field hitters. Hitting to the opposite field behind a base runner is invaluable, especially on the hit and run play.

HE DID NOT consider Ted Williams to be nearly as great a batsman as he could have been. The defensive shift of outfielders and even infielders on Williams could be easily defeated, said Cobb, if Williams cared to defeat it. And Cobb was right. Frank Thomas, of the New York Mets, is regarded as a dead left-field hitter, and by nature he is. However, this same Thomas can hit to right field if he wishes, enough, anyhow, to keep the defense honest, and he can teach the move to any batsman. True, the batter sacrifices some power in this movement, and power hitters, including Thomas, hate to make that sacrifice. The home-run appeal, with the record frequency kept on the cuff, means money in the opinion of many power hitters, and unfortunately they are too frequently right. Most power hitters would rather gamble for the home run over their own fence than for the single or double so openly offered. Not Cobb. He would be grossly insulted if an outfield were to shift for him.

One more word on Cobb on the subject of his hitting. I may have left the impression that Cobb was not a power hitter. On several occasions he would engage in a pre-game exhibition contest of power hitting. It is said that he never lost a single contest. He could drive a ball for tremendous distance when that was his only purpose. I don't believe that Cobb, when batting, ever had a home run in his mind.

Adventure was always inviting to him, almost compelling. The percentage could be low, but if the chance was present at all, he would take it. He caused catchers to call for more pitch-outs by far than any player in the history of the game, thereby setting up constantly the three-and-one and two-and-nothing situations for the next batsman and giving repeated opportunity for the batsman to hit the "cripple." However, he had no such altruistic purpose in his mind. He was not at all what you would call a team player in the sense that he had any consideration whatever for the record or standing of another player. He was an independent. He was thinking of running —of a stolen base, of two stolen bases. He was in reality thinking of beating somebody at something—right now and always.

As a realist, he was completely selfish. Tyrus Raymond had to win. In a game of tiddlywinks with his own son, he would lose his temper in defeat. He would not cheat him, no, but he could not endure a loss. He did not care to play a game he could not win. Cobb was a professional deluxe. There was no recognition in his soul for sport for sport's sake. There must be the element of gain for himself.

There are so many incidents, large and small, that are very vivid in my memory and that help draw the character of this man. As an invited guest of Wilbert Robinson, the venerable catcher and manager at Baltimore and Brooklyn, on Robinson's hunting estate in Georgia, Cobb gobbled up all the game. He could easily out-walk Uncle Robbie, and he charged every point of quail, coveys or singles, leaving the heavy, trodding Uncle Robbie without a shot. Robinson told me the story with a touch of humor but utter dismay. The fact that Cobb had already bagged the limit for both hunters did not slacken his rush for the next flush. Cobb simply had to be first. He could—and did—censure one of his first minor-league roommates, Nap Rucker, if he took the first bath. He would not stand for that.

I am giving illustrative facts about Cobb that may seem discreditable, but only to give a correct portrayal of the man. Facts are facts—and Cobb is Cobb. Some facts about Cobb could mislead one's judgment. It seems to me that there can be a difference between detailed facts and the overall truth. Cobb is to be understood rather than maligned unjustly. The truth is that Cobb is the greatest one-game player in all baseball history. He was the most positive character in the game. He was baseball's most earnest and assidu-ous learner. He was the greatest perfectionist both on offense and defense.

No player could come close to Cobb's record. Probably no one will ever equal it.

BATTING AVERAGE	.367
GAMES	3,033
RUNS	2,244
HITS	4,191
STOLEN BASES	892

Cobb was competitively unbalanced, but the truth is that his baseball immortality will stand forever. Cobb died a wealthy man, wealthier than any other player in the professional game, including Spalding. He left a goodly sum for college scholarships to worthy boys. He enlarged and endowed the hospital in his old home town.

Who's the greatest player that ever performed in the major leagues? The vote would surely be Cobb or Wagner. Take your pick. Cobb had a psychological effect on opponents which Wagner did not have. Wagner had a morale value among his teammates which Cobb did not have. If I had first chance in making up an all-time All-American team *for a season's play of 154 games,* I would be compelled to choose Wagner. But for *the* game today: Ty Cobb.

Ty Cobb was a pitcher's nemesis when on base. He stole second, third and home in one inning on three occasions.

Connie Mack

CORNELIUS MCGILLICUDDY was born of Irish immigrant parents in East Brookfield, Massachusetts, in 1862. He attended school under that name. He signed it on the shoe-factory payroll as a teen-aged worker when he took his earnings home to his widowed mother. But the long name was abbreviated when his sandlot and semiprofessional catching drew a following that shortened it to Connie Mack. And Connie Mack it remained through three generations of baseball history until the entire nation and its President mourned his passing at the age of ninety-three. However, to me, twenty years younger, he was always "Mr. Mack," and so I write it that way.

A long and distinguished career as manager and owner has clouded the fact that for a decade—from 1886—he was one of the game's great catchers. He first drew attention as a player of twenty in 1883 when he caught for the East Brookfield team that won the championship of central Massachusetts. He turned professional the next year as catcher for nearby Meriden of the Connecticut State League. His reputation brought him a contract in 1886 from Washington, where he caught for four years. He joined the Brotherhood movement in 1890 and set a record for durability by catching 123 of Buffalo's 132 games. Following the demise of the Players League, his contract was assigned to Pittsburgh. There he was player-manager until 1896.

Through the influence and persuasion of pioneering Ban Johnson and Charles Comiskey, Mr. Mack signed as manager of Milwaukee in Johnson's Western League for 1897, and there began the Mack wizardry with and understanding of players. Milwaukee was never lower than fourth place in the four years of his management. He also succeeded financially, for, when Johnson was ready to rename his league the American League and move toward major status, Mr. Mack was ready to open a new location in the great expansion of big-league baseball.

Again through the sponsorship of Johnson and Comiskey, Mr. Mack took over the Philadelphia franchise as part owner and manager. He brought a formidable team of Athletics home fourth in 1901 and first in 1902. Most of his better players were recruited from the National League, which had made itself vulnerable to raiding by setting a salary limit (in 1892) of $2,400. The reserve clause in the players' contracts at that time was regarded as valid. Litigation between the two leagues followed, and players could not with impunity disregard it. The scope of the defection is reflected in the Athletics' player roster of 1902, almost all selected from the National League. Selecting this championship list placed Mr. Mack at the top as a team balancer, meaning one who builds a team as an entity with the same judgment that a good scout selects individual players. No team could tolerate the eccentric George Edward "Rube" Waddell, but Mr. Mack had managed the left-hander in Milwaukee and willingly took him from the Chicago Nationals. He could handle all types. He could get the top mark of effort out of a Waddell or a finished gentleman like Herb Pennock. The Rube won ninety-five games for him in the next four years.

MR. MACK gave me an insight into his methods during an enjoyable month of travel in Texas in the 1919 spring training of the Athletics and the St. Louis Cardinals. There was a certain kinship, for we were both going through the mill with young and inexperienced players. He was poor, as I was. So he accepted my invitation to train with me and my Cardinal team in Brownsville, Texas, and we played our series of games in five different cities in the Rio Grande valley—San Benito, Harlingen, Donna, Farr, and McAllen. We also played games in Brownsville, and the boys had their escapades over in Matamoros across the river—his and mine too. I don't think we ever did know all the facts, but we knew enough. I came to know all the players on both teams. There were not any really "bad" boys.

Anyway, after the day's game, we would sit together in the old pullman car on a siding or in a frontier hotel lobby and we would talk together about our players—about trades, coaches and tactics, and team building. Murphy, his signal-relay man, was intriguingly clever and good for extended comment after every game. Murphy was a good man at stealing signals. In fact, Mr. Mack's whole team was a signal-stealing team. It was in these talks that I got my first idea on how to get, but more particularly how to give, signals. Years later, Mr. Mack was terribly hurt when he lost his relay man. He told me he just couldn't get anyone to handle the relay. He came to manage from the bench more than any man in baseball,

Connie Mack

Mr. Mack, my greatest friend in baseball.

unless it be McGraw in his later years. I can remember many little stories he would tell, too, of his handling his men. I must tell just one.

In complaining about a ten-dollar fine Mr. Mack had assessed on Ossie Schreckingost for his second late arrival for a meeting, the famous catcher, who was Rube Waddell's roommate, said: "Rube didn't come to the meeting at all, and you didn't fine him."

"Now, lookit, Ossie," Mr. Mack replied, "if you want me to treat you as we do George Edward, we will do just that."

"Oh, no, no, Mr. Mack!" Ossie exclaimed, "I don't want that." And Ossie left, penitent and satisfied.

This was one of many examples of how Mr. Mack would exercise his marvelous control and guidance of diversified personalities. He worked in such a way that there was never a chance for a feud on his club. Mr. Mack was a "meeting" manager, and one of the first. But even discipline had its choice definition in his control of players. He wanted his men to have such regard for physical fitness that they would impose upon themselves those restrictions or practices that kept them at top condition for winning games. He believed that no real discipline was obtained unless it was self-imposed and voluntary. Here was Mr. Mack's highest contribution to team morale. Every man was his own manager in his desire for knowledge and physical fitness. That was, and still is, the uncharted but everlasting influence of Mr. Mack's teaching. This is his immortality.

The pleasing manner of Mr. Mack quickly developed wide player affection for himself, and almost as quickly would come profound respect for his technical knowledge of individual play and sound tactics. He was a kindly pedagogue. He liked boys, and all were mere boys, and they liked him. When they left him they felt that they had been in the presence of a minister. But Mr. Mack's policy of trying to have all his associates, players and staff, assume extended responsibility for his own success did not mean "every man on his own." Not every boy can be left on his own. He was firm with the wayward players, but regarded all deportment as individualistic.

It has been said that the greatest single qualification of a successful baseball manager is the ability to handle men. Mr. Mack had that, of course, because he had the two ingredients that produce the ability: mastery of the art of private conversation, and the willingness to use it.

Within a few years of selecting his Athletics of 1901, Mr. Mack began replacing age with youth from what is called the "free-agency field," that is, players with no previous experience in organized baseball. In that day good colleges offered the most prospects, and Mr. Mack signed a number of players directly from college. Among these were Eddie Plank from Gettysburg College; Chief Bender, Carlisle Indian School; Eddie Collins, Columbia University; Jack Barry, Holy Cross; and Jack Coombs, Colby College. During that period he found and developed Frank "Home Run" Baker, Stuffy McInnis, Amos Strunk, Rube Oldring, Andy Coakley, and others. The result was a new team of Athletics that won pennants and World Series in 1910, 1911, and 1913. After winning the American League pennant again in 1914 and then losing the World Series to the Boston Braves in four straight games, Mr. Mack began to dismantle his great team. During this dispersal of stars, and even after, Mr. Mack believed firmly that, without extended delay, he could build a new great club. I happen to know that he had great confidence in himself for the reconstruction. He had never employed salaried scouts to rival the production staffs of other clubs. In fact, I believe that the Athletics spent less on formal scouting than any other club in either league, due in part to Mr. Mack's continued expectations of strong recruits from the free-agency field. His history of employment of boys with limited professional experience, or, indeed, none at all, gave him the full right to believe in himself, and his record changed the views of many managers about the readiness and ability of free-agent players to step into the majors as regulars without any previous minor-league service. I was one of those.

I am sure that every major-league manager, past or present, can bring to mind a roster of players whom he regretfully disregarded and who went elsewhere and made good. Surely no manager had a lower percentage of such unconditionally released players than Mr. Mack. I do not know of a single such player so released by him. But his quantity production was comparatively nil. From 1915 through 1921 the Athletics finished last. Then they were seventh, sixth, and fifth. He endured continuous surprise in the failures of his teams. He suffered disappointment in efforts that had formerly wrought spectacular successes. But no longer could he find the free agents that had been so plentiful. True, he had an occasional star—Ed Rommel, for example, and the versatile Jimmy Dykes—but there were never enough to give him a balanced team. Competition had increased. The St. Louis farm-system idea was developing fast.

Mr. Mack's sky lost its nimbus clouds after 1924. He finished second in 1925 and third in 1926. He made a personal alliance with Jack Dunn, owner of the Baltimore Orioles and six-time champion of the International League. But he had resorted to the use of cash. Dunn sold him

Max Bishop in 1924, and Lefty Grove the next year for $100,500. He bought Al Simmons from Milwaukee and, for 1925, Mickey Cochrane from the Portland, Oregon, club, of which the Athletics were part owners. He took on Jimmy Foxx, an untried teen-ager, on the recommendation of Home Run Baker. Then Joe Boley came from Baltimore, as did George Earnshaw.

The onrushing Athletics of the mid-1920's caught and passed the Ruth-Gehrig Yankees in late 1928, but only for a day or two, and then they lost out. But everyone knew that the Athletics were the coming team. Mr. Mack never built for one year. The Athletics arrived and began to dominate the American League by winning 313 games in 1929, 1930, and 1931. They won the World Series in the first two years and lost to my Cardinals in 1931. Within two years Mr. Mack began selling the stars of this, his third great club, to satisfy the pressing need of cash as the great depression of the early 1930's pinched him and his partners, the Shibe brothers. The team plunged into the second division and remained there for several years.

During this period, Mr. Mack gradually became a convert to the player-production pos- sibilities of the farm system. He was elected president of the Athletics in 1937. Three years later he bought control from the Shibe family. At age eighty-two he began a somewhat desperate reconstruction job, only to be confronted a year later by a world war that devoured manpower and kept it at a premium for more than five years. We met more than occasionally, and each time he told me of his discouragement. He did not have enough available cash to enter the purchasing market with several carelessly wealthy competi- tors of the postwar period. This was distressing to all his friends, for his work and career did not deserve this fate. He was and is worthy of study and imitation by all baseball managers, major or minor, college, semipro, Little League, all of us!

Mr. Mack retired in 1950. Four years later the historic park bearing his name was sold to the rival Phillies. He sold his Athletics to a Mid- western business syndicate. The team was moved to Kansas City, where it has remained in the second division. The team is gone, but the warm- ing memory of this great and gentle man will always remain in Philadelphia, as it has since his passing in 1956. And baseball will be grateful always for what he has meant to the game.

Judge Kenesaw Mountain Landis

IN THE dark winter of 1920, baseball was in a panic as a result of evidence of crookedness assembled by the American League presi- dent, Ban Johnson. Eight Chicago White Sox players had conspired to throw the 1919 World Series. Professional baseball managers and owners were full of fear that public confidence in the great national game was jeopardized, if not lost.

"Oh, Lord, anybody!" was the prayerful atti- tude of every owner in the game. "Anybody who can save us."

Attention had been called some years before (1906) to a forty-year-old federal judge, Kenesaw Mountain Landis. He had fined the Standard Oil Company $29,240,000 in a freight-rebate case, and this gave him wide and favorable publicity. In 1915 and 1916 the same Judge Landis had earned the gratitude of organized baseball with his han- dling of the "outlaw" Federal League's action to enjoin the National and American Leagues. Landis took the suit under advisement in January 1915 and withheld a decision until the two major leagues could arrange a peace with the Federals, which they did two years later. As a result, organized baseball was saved from any possible adverse decision.

In late 1920, organized baseball offered to Landis a job as supervisor of the game, to be known as the commissioner of baseball. The terms of the contract, dictated by Landis, gave the commissioner despotic power in all directions. He could do anything he pleased in the dis- ciplinary field, whether it involved players, um- pires, club owners, or club employees.

Whatever the terms of the contract submitted by Judge Landis might have been, it would have been, at that time, accepted by baseball. The future depended on who the dictator was.

LANDIS was a lover of the game, on the field and off. To him it was the national game, demanding protection. That made him a meticulous guardian. His first move proved it. Without compassion he put every man implicated

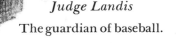

Judge Landis

The guardian of baseball.

White Sox players during the 1919 Series, Ban Johnson began a strenuous, forceful, and uncompromising investigation to get the facts. He risked and lost the long-standing friendship of his partner and sponsor, Charles Comiskey. The two had practically run the American League for twenty years. Yet the White Sox owner simply resented any action by anyone on only rumors against the boys he had brought into the big league. He could not see a scintilla of reason for suspicion. But Johnson persisted. He produced irrefutable evidence of guilt and proposed that the charges be brought into civil court. He insisted upon this procedure.

At this point Commissioner Landis, whose contract gave him exclusive authority to handle all matters pertaining to "conduct detrimental to baseball," stepped into the limelight. His position was, "We don't need the law courts. I can handle this matter and I will. And you, Mr. Johnson, can step out of the picture. I don't need your help." Then followed the beginning of a deep animosity between Johnson and Landis. Johnson had opposed the Landis contract, which did, indeed, affect the disciplinary rights and authority of the major-league presidents. Deprivation of his formerly unlimited control resulted in Johnson's downright viciousness toward Landis.

This attitude was reciprocated blow for blow. The feud was resolved only when American League club owners, as an alternative to the commissioner's impending resignation, turned against their founder and president and stripped him of power. Johnson was removed from all previously held functions, all except the purely administrative tasks of his league office.

Regardless of personalities and clashes, organized baseball did obtain a satisfactory answer to its dire need of the moment. The integrity of the federal court was behind professional baseball. *Public confidence and faith in the game was now firm.*

Commissioner Landis was a baseball fan. He attended major-league games in many cities, especially Chicago. He believed very firmly at all times that baseball had an important place in the recreational life of our country. It is to be hoped that baseball has not forgotten the words of Judge Landis, uttered in 1916 and seemingly in defense of his delay on the Federal League suit: "Both sides may understand that any blows at the thing called baseball would be regarded by this court as a blow to a national institution."

It would be well for the stewards of organized baseball today, and, indeed, the Congress of the United States, to heed the wisdom of Judge Landis as expressed about a half century ago.

in the White Sox scandal out of baseball forever. Risberg, Cicotte, Gandil, McMullin, Felsch, Weaver, Williams, and Jackson. At no point did he temper justice with mercy. And today who is there to say that he did not act wisely?

It is an imponderable assertion that Joe Jackson could have continued in baseball without disturbing public confidence. There may have been admissions by Jackson to which neither the player nor the public gave proper consideration. That Chick Gandil, for example, could have said in effect, to Jackson, "If we lose this series, Joe, there's a lot of money we can make," and that Jackson entirely resented it by making up his simple mind to play his best. And that he did! His .375 batting average was highest of both teams, and he hit the only home run in the series.

There must have been no extenuating circumstances to mitigate his permanent banishment. However, neither the ignorant Jackson nor the sympathetic public believed he was ever dishonest in play. In any event, one of the three all-time outfielders was forever banned.

It is undisputed that as soon as rumors were heard of dishonesty on the part of the Chicago

William J. Klem

EDICATION is a one-word description of William J. Klem throughout his thirty-six years as a National League umpire. After officiating in well over 5,000 regular-season games and eighteen World Series, he often claimed with pride, "I never called one wrong." Then, pointing to the region of his heart, he would add, "Not in here!"

To the baseball public, he fairly symbolized the game's honesty in behalf of an equally devoted corps of unsung officials whose spotless integrity extends back through a century of baseball. Perhaps this little-known episode in the fourth year of Klem's National League service will help explain the public's justifiable faith in umpires.

Klem was alone in the umpires' dressing room under the grandstand of the Polo Grounds on October 6, 1908. In relating the story to an old friend of mine, Bill McKechnie, of the Baseball Hall of Fame, Klem explained that his pre-game thoughts centered around a fervent hope that, as plate umpire of this all-important contest, there would be no occasion for him to run any player of either team off the field. The Polo Grounds had overflowed with fans. Excitement and tension were high. The winner would win the 1908 pennant, for it was the historic re-play of the tie game of September 23 between the Chicago Cubs and the New York Giants, who had finished in a tie.

Suddenly a complete stranger entered the umpires' dressing room. He stood before Klem with a large roll of paper money, all five-dollar bills, visible.

"Here's four thousand dollars!" he said. "You are officiating today's game—"

"Get out!" Klem roared. "You get out!"

I like to think that Bill's muscles reacted before his brain got any message, because he made no effort to learn the man's identity, or which team was to be favored. No one in quest of the Holy Grail could be more pure in his pursuit than was Bill Klem in protecting the basic structure of baseball, its utter integrity. Almost instinctively he grabbed the intruder's coat collar and literally threw him out of the dressing room, reflecting, I believe, the quick reaction of all umpires.

To a writer once seeking humorous recollections from a long and sometimes controversial career, Klem replied, "Young man, there is *nothing* funny about baseball umpiring."

"Come on, Bill!" the writer persisted. "Do you mean to say you have watched the crazy antics of managers and players all afternoon and then, reaching your hotel room, you never enjoyed laughing at them?"

"Never!" Klem intoned solemnly. "Never on the same day!"

He had a sense of humor, and a keen one, behind his grim façade. Otherwise, how could he face up to a recalcitrant and declare in haughty rebuttal, *"You,* sir, are a muttonhead!"

Legend assures us that there was no love lost between Klem and manager John J. McGraw. But history indicates plenty of respect that must have been mutual. On April 25, 1913, when the Giants were starting after their third straight pennant, Klem had occasion to cancel a game-winning single in the tenth with the bases full, against Philadelphia, at the Polo Grounds, because, at the moment of the pitch, *his back was turned to the plate.* He ordered another pitch and the Giant batter, McCormick, hit into a double play. The game ended in a tie an inning later.

The partisan crowd yelled and became unruly, but John McGraw made no protest. Klem had turned to announce the pinch hitter, McCormick. The pitcher should never have thrown the ball. An umpire cannot call what he does not see, and Klem stuck to the rules, under the worst possible circumstances. A few months later McGraw selected Klem as best in the National League to join the Giants and White Sox that Fall in their round-the-world tour.

Klem was born in Rochester, New York, on February 22, 1874, of German-born parents. The family name was Klimm, which Bill changed legally shortly after becoming a National League umpire in 1905, his first season. The veteran umpire Hank O'Day introduced him to league president Harry Pulliam, but another veteran umpire, Bob Emslie, took young Klem in tow and sponsored him over many rough spots during his beginning years.

Klem more than repaid his early benefactor when advancing years caught up with him. "Bill kept me in the league for eight years," Emslie revealed, "by working behind the plate for me, even through both games of double-headers in the heat of summer."

Klem's National League career began just about the time the major leagues decided to employ the two-umpire system. The "chief" worked

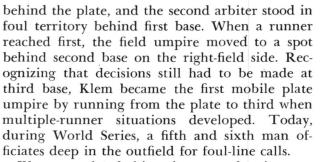

behind the plate, and the second arbiter stood in foul territory behind first base. When a runner reached first, the field umpire moved to a spot behind second base on the right-field side. Recognizing that decisions still had to be made at third base, Klem became the first mobile plate umpire by running from the plate to third when multiple-runner situations developed. Today, during World Series, a fifth and sixth man officiates deep in the outfield for foul-line calls.

Klem completed thirty-six years of active umpiring in 1940 at the age of sixty-six, when he was appointed chief of the National League's umpiring staff. The year brought honors in several cities, where "Bill Klem nights" became festive tributes. Thereafter much of his supervision was done in the press box, which he preferred, until his retirement to his Florida home. He was hospitalized in September 1951 and died on the 16th at the age of seventy-seven. He was survived only by his wife, Marie, but mourned by the entire baseball world.

The record of the umpiring profession, an honorable one indeed, does not permit the selection of one or a few to be singled out as an exceptional example. There is no place to stop when the only consideration is a single virtue, such as honesty or the many high requisites of umpiring. But Bill Klem had faultless technical qualities for umpir-

Bill Klem

The master umpire—over 5,000 games.

ing: the timing of the decision; the call; the raised right fist for emphasis and visible information; the adaptation of voice or gesture to fit the occasion or tension; the "inside" crouch between catcher and batter; the inherent love of the game; the jealous stewardship of its good name and lasting reputation; the discreet and forceful handling of players and managers and, indeed, the public.

All these qualities, and more, combined into one person resulted in William J. Klem, and he fused them with a lifetime of dedication.

J. G. Taylor Spink

J. G. TAYLOR SPINK took over the publication of *The Sporting News* in 1914, when he was twenty-five years old. The untimely death of his father dumped the weekly baseball journal into his lap overnight. Since 1886, this periodical, supervised by Taylor's uncle and then by his father, had been the weekly newsletter of all professional baseball clubs. For its first fifty years, it offered the only scouting information available to professional baseball.

During the entire period of its publication it has taken an influential part in all issues involving the integrity and future of the game. *The Sporting News* supported the expansion to two leagues in 1900, opposed the Federal League in 1914, deplored the bonus orgy and still does, and has seldom taken a neutral position in any controversy. It has had a bold and assertive conscience in matters where advancement of the game was concerned, and the heart core of policy making was for thirty-seven years in the hands of one man and one man only—J. G. Taylor Spink.

Baseball itself, professional I mean, owes the crown of immortality to Taylor Spink. Most thinking individuals past and present will heartily approve my recognition of Taylor Spink as highly worthy of baseball immortality. He was gruff, in manner and in tone and in language. He was ruled by his meticulous sense of duty. A great United States general said that the word "duty" was the most sublime word in the English language. Well, Taylor Spink had it. He also had several other words that would have enhanced the conversational vocabulary of a disgruntled imbibing sea gob. But it was a rough and unrealistic exterior, a rather deep camouflage. He was kindly in front of sorrow or distress. He was secretively but lavishly generous in meeting need where it was personal—not corporate or in the mass. He was a barking dog, but he could, he might, he would bite on occasion.

He never ran for cover.

Taylor Spink was a businessman, a tireless, self-demanding taskmaster of himself and everybody else. He seemed to get a lot of joy out of pursuit—no, not exactly joy, for he never seemed to catch it. But he had a gluesome stick-to-itiveness to whatever he was doing, and "doing" was a lifetime assignment of atrocious daily hours of work —work with a secretary, a pen and paper, numerous assistants, but particularly the telephone and telegraph office. He seemed to be always chasing his objective, which, in turn, seemed to Taylor never quite to be caught. The chase had no start. It existed beforehand.

He was a newspaper publisher, a primeval publisher who delegated nothing to anybody, unless it was accompanied by explicit procedural instruction. Help did almost all of the actual or original writing, but Taylor edited all articles for all his publications, changed the substance rather than the style, and frequently substituted his name for the author's. He had come to feel that he had actually written the story. He had no classical education. He never started in that direction, yet he could write surprisingly well. Sinclair Lewis would have classed Taylor as a genius in literary attainment, for Taylor qualified in Lewis's definition of genius in writers—he wore out the seat of his pants on a chair bottom.

TAYLOR was a self-made publisher, which in some cases would be a doubtful compliment. He knew he was self-made, as he put it, and he thanked no one for his personal achievements. He took responsibility for everything before it happened. He never second-guessed himself. He controlled all the ifs in a complex and at times very turbulent business. He enjoyed praise, and he could deceive himself in seeking commendation.

One of his credit cards for admission to baseball immortality was his devotion to the health and best interests of the game. Baseball was an extremely jealous mistress to J. G. Taylor Spink. It may be that he will never be elected to the Baseball Hall of Fame, but he would have my vote, and time (perhaps the long time) is his tenderest ally. I believe the game itself may rise up a generation hence and with belated unanimity accord an honor long since actually earned.

Edward G. Barrow

THE MOST underestimated man on the professional baseball horizon of the past seventy-five years was Edward G. Barrow. He made no statistical records. Of humble birth, he became baseball's most comprehensive contributor in all the many departments of the game save one—he was never a major-league player. As a young man, he played baseball, managing as a boy, and became one of the great major-league managers and a World Series winner. He had the esteem in the early years of Charles Comiskey, Ban Johnson, Connie Mack, and others of like prominence. He came to have effective influence in the later years with all baseball people from Commissioner Landis on down to the minor leagues. He had more power behind the scenes of baseball politics than any one single person in the game over a period of twenty-five years. Very few ever knew it.

He was baseball's modest but leading entrepreneur, never afraid of innovations. He had the first woman player in baseball, Lizzie (Arlington) Stroud. She pitched for him in Wilmington. He had the first night game in the minor leagues. They couldn't finish it, but he had it. The famous Fred Clarke as a very young boy helped Ed Barrow distribute morning newspapers in Des Moines. He brought the boy into the professional game of baseball. He employed Zane Grey, the writer, as a professional player on his Wilmington club. As manager, Ed Barrow won two pennants in a single season—in two leagues. He met Harry Stevens, father of the Stevens Brothers, the present concession empire, in Columbus, Ohio, when he was a young man twenty-six years of age, and he became a partner of Mr. Stevens for a time. That close acquaintanceship lasted for his lifetime. He never lost friends. They made an adventure into the theatrical business together, but that experience brought Ed Barrow back to baseball. He brought Honus Wagner into the professional game at Paterson, New Jersey, at a salary of $125 per month. He was responsible for Nick Altrock's advance to Toronto. He brought Cy Seymour into the profession as a pitcher and changed him into an outfielder. Seymour could not get pitching control because he had short fingers. He was the early confidant of Ban Johnson, and through Johnson, Barrow engineered the transfer of Miller Huggins from the management of the St. Louis Nationals to the Yankees. He brought Arthur Devlin and Moose McCormack into Indianapolis. He changed Babe Ruth from pitcher to outfielder. He brought Ruth and Mays to New York. He was

able to select the best player scouts in the country, and he maintained this scouting staff for a period of twenty-five years in New York. John L. Sullivan and James A. Corbett belonged to the army of friendly scouts whose reference to players was always a source of player supply to Barrow. Corbett umpired for him. So did John L., for one day.

IT IS NOT generally known that Ed Barrow was really the discoverer of Ty Cobb. He made the first money offer to the Augusta club, for Ty Cobb and Joe Engel, but was beat by a few hundred dollars. Cobb got nothing, but the club got $1,500.

Ed Barrow was a player scout, none better. He knew what to look for in the early qualifications. His investigation always went beyond hitting, running, and throwing. His final estimate on player ability was positive tops. He was the key man in counsel that placed Connie Mack as a major-league manager at Milwaukee in the American League, and from there Mr. Mack went to Philadelphia as part owner and manager. He changed the old Atlantic League to the Eastern League and got AA rating. He organized the International League and became its president for several years. In other words, Ed Barrow is partially responsible for the present and enduring International League.

He became manager of the Boston Americans and won the 1918 pennant and World Series. He brought George Weiss from New Haven to the Yankees, where George succeeded Mr. Barrow as a really great general manager. And it can be said that a new list of immortals, twenty-five years hence, will include George Weiss, when he shall have left the Metropolitan Baseball Club of New York a repeated pennant winner.

Great as Barrow was in accuracy of judgment of individual players, his team-balancing ability was even more distinctive. It is indeed a risky business to put the dollar mark on the individual muscle. It is something to know quickly that a youngster has a prospective future of great excellence. It is an entirely different challenge to judge forty men as a team, as an expressive entity, as a unit of efficient play calculated to excel seven other competitive clubs. He was never deceived or delayed by the "anesthetic" player—good enough for the manager not to know that twenty-five such men would finish in the second division. Such a manager would say, "I am all right at that position," but that decision is a year too late. Barrow believed that the greatest weakness of managers was to include an anesthetic in the club make-up. It was far better, in his opinion, to get rid of a good player a year too soon than to hold a poor player a year too long. In the first instance, the error was one of judgment, said he, based on the erroneous belief that another player was available equally as good or better and so the release was not harmful. In the second case, he would be taken by surprise, unprepared and with no prospect for substitution.

TEAM BALANCING is really a study in art. To have the component department of a club properly related involves a thorough knowledge of both front-line and bench strength. Barrow was able to accept, say, unavoidable mediocre speed and to offset it by superstrength in power batting or cagey pitching. Team balancing is a problem that faces general management constantly and whose proper solution produces championships. That's where Barrow steps front and center.

Ed Barrow was the greatest student and master of team balancing of any man I ever knew. He accounts for the Yankee regime, and he left it in good hands.

McGraw was not in any sense a scout. He was a team balancer in the sense that he made the most of what he had. He was not a producer of players. Connie Mack had no paid scouting staff—well, hardly any. Neither had many players to select from. Barrow was different. He was a producer, but above all a team balancer. For years and years he had no serious ups and downs in league standings. He was ahead of the grandstand critic in divining a year ahead of the public that player X was marketable. It takes great self-confidence and judgment to get rid of a popular player, but the stability of a winning team requires *that* kind of managerial risk constantly. That self-confidence and judgment Ed Barrow had. It was his personal scouting ability together with his finding and employment of three or four great scouts and George Weiss that gave him quality players in excess of need, and it was Ed's ability behind the scenes that balanced the Yankee team for continued championships.

He would handle the league president and Commissioner Landis to the queen's taste, and he seldom got his name or face in the paper. He was baseball's Mark Hanna. He would sit obscurely in the open seats, way back in the grandstand, and while he wanted to win, of course, the score was not the gripping objective. He was so interested in the trees, he couldn't at the moment contemplate

Ed Barrow

The man who found Wagner and Cobb and who brought Babe Ruth to New York.

the beauty of the woods.

The Yankee dynasty of superiority was not an accident of ownership or sagacity of managers or the luck of scouts or the prestige of the city name or the reputation of "Yankee." It was the wise production of players and fixing of team identity by Ed Barrow. He knew what he needed and he knew what to do with it when he got it. I doubt that sportswriters of the country have ever appreciated fully the originality and importance of Ed Barrow. I doubt if many baseball celebrities knew about his industry or his thorough planning-ahead. In a grandstand visit during a game with him, he would quietly tell me the changes that confronted the Yankees as much as two years into the future. It was baseball education at its best to sit with him for two hours or so, if on rare occasion he would let his hair down and talk, watching the Yankees and hearing his comments on his own players and the other team's. Knowledge of the other team was important to him, second only to knowledge of his own.

A repeating winning club is not miraculous. It comes from job devotion and knowing players and above all putting them together properly. Ed Barrow was the number one man in my baseball acquaintance for making and maintaining a winning club.

Babe Ruth

"HIYA, KEED," was his usual greeting. He called the whole world "kid." If he knew you for ten years or ten minutes he would never remember you or your name, so everyone had one name. Kid.

The great torso and the massive round face with the ringlets of black hair, the big spread nose and the brown eyes. The face everyone has seen. The face everyone knows. The face of George Herman Ruth for one generation, perhaps for two, became the face of baseball in America.

And this was the man who changed the game on one word: *power!* He was called *The Babe*—and he was a physical prodigy. His bodily reflexes were instant and superior. He almost reveled in them. He didn't care if people thought he overdid the lustiness. It made no difference to him what people thought about anything. *They* couldn't hit home runs. He didn't know the names of many of his teammates. He didn't care to know them. *They* couldn't hit home runs. He lived most of his life close to the rocks of intellectual indifference, and the easily observable marks of culture were few.

Waite Hoyt, a teammate of Ruth's at both Boston and New York, probably knew Ruth better and more intimately than anyone else. He wrote a brief biographical article on Ruth, a revealing character study equal in effect to Boswell's *Johnson*. Two incidents described in Hoyt's article are typical of the Babe's career:

When Marshal Foch, the Commander of all the Allied forces of World War One, visited here in 1921, he was received in New York with open arms. The usual reception at City Hall. Ticker tape and confetti floated from the office windows. It was summer, and Marshal Foch had been persuaded to attend his first baseball game. The Yankees were then still tenants of the Polo Grounds and it was the Yankee team which was to play host to the world-famous hero. At two forty-five, the motor cavalcade bearing the Marshal drew near the Polo Grounds. The park was bedecked with French and American Flags. The stands were crowded. The line of autos came through the center field gates. The band played the Star Spangled Banner and the Marseillaise. The crowd rose to its feet. As Marshal Foch alighted from his motor car and stepped into Col. Ruppert's private box, the players lined up at attention to one side of the Yankee bench. He was attired in a powder blue French uniform, with myriad battle ribbons and insignia pinned to his chest. We, the ball players, were to have the privilege of shaking hands with the great French Marshal. Babe Ruth was to be our master of ceremonies. He was there to make the speech of welcome on behalf of the ball players.

When it was time for Ruth to speak, the crowd was hushed. Marshal Foch bent over to catch Ruth's words. They were slow in coming, as the Babe was flustered. Finally he managed to blurt, "Hey, Gen., they tell me you were in the war."

A similar incident occurred at the Yankee Stadium later in the twenties. Cal Coolidge was President of the United States. Just before one game, word reached the bench that President Coolidge was arriving. Once again we were to line up to meet a dignitary. Once again Ruth was to speak for the ball players. We filed by shaking hands with Mr. Coolidge. Babe Ruth finally arrived in front of the quiet-mannered President. Ruth was again flabbergasted. He whipped out a big, red bandana handkerchief, mopped his face, and snorted, "Hot as hell, ain't it, Pres?"

President Coolidge sat down. Presidents and bat boys—they were all alike to the Bambino.

BABE RUTH is known to the press and public of this country chiefly as a home-run hitter. He was very much more than that. He could run and field, both above average, and had an extraordinarily strong arm. In fact, he had the playing aptitudes and qualities of a Wagner. He could play any position. But his physical prowess dominated and led to practically every distinction that came to him. He had a bodily capacity for life's selectives faster and fuller than most. He could not live a single minute simply as a breathing person. His physiological appetites sought instant, persistent, and enduring satisfaction. His was the life of pursuit—vibrant joy in the chase. He never gave thought to tomorrow. He lived for today, now—for the very next stroke of the bat.

However, he was a rational conservative in play as compared to Cobb, but a very positive force on the field. There was a surcharged atmosphere of interest with Ruth anywhere visible in uniform. He enjoyed the game. He would have played for nothing rather than not play at all.

Babe Ruth never knew a mother or a father. He never had a home. As a youth, he was a community dependent. Perhaps these early deprivations caused him to have the all-redemptive quality of loving children, and he was almost equal to Leo Durocher in having all children love him. Wherever he might be or whatever he might be doing, he could always become very quickly "as a little child." I can think of Babe Ruth en-

Babe Ruth

For two generations and perhaps more, the Babe was the face of baseball in America.

ROBERT RIGER

tering Heaven upon that simple Biblical requirement.

Babe Ruth changed the game in some directions more than any other person. Surely second in all directions only to Mr. Byron Bancroft Johnson.

He made the home-run record in 1927, a year when the American League hit less than one-third of the home runs recorded by the American League in 1961. Let's be exact about the facts.

Ruth, in 1927, hit sixty home runs. The American League, in 1927, hit a total of 439 home runs.

The American League, in 1961, hit 1534 home runs. Therefore, on the basis of this calculation, Ruth would have hit 209 home runs in 1961 ($439 \div 60 = 1534 \div 209.66$).

Any American League batsman hitting sixty home runs in 1961 would have hit, in 1927, on the basis of this calculation, seventeen home runs ($1534 \div 60 = 439 \div 17.21$).

Some allowance must be made in Ruth's disfavor, changing the figures slightly, on account of the increase in season games from 154 in 1927 to 162 in 1961. This change would not be very substantial and could be made exact by subtracting the number of home runs hit in the American League in the added eight games in 1961.

The ten leading home-run hitters in the American League in 1927, excluding Ruth and Gehrig, hit a total of 124 home runs, which is an average of 12.4 per man.

The ten leading home-run hitters in the American League, in 1961, excluding Maris and Mantle, hit a total of 341 home runs, which is an average of 34.1 per man.

Is it credible that, within the short period of twenty-four years in the history of the human race, young men had increased their physical power threefold? If so, it is credible that another twenty-four progressive years would bring us to a team of supermen, every man a mythological Hercules.

Ruth's power at chart glance would permit any competent baseball judge to classify most of the present power hitters in the majors as mere boys, compared to Ruth. A heavy forty-six-ounce bat swished like a wisp of straw covered more footage in its sweep from start to finish than that of any player who ever lived.

So much for the home-run record. In what way has Ruth changed the game? In the course of a few years, Ruth more than anyone else made the stolen base an antiquated feature of professional baseball. Unfortunately, that great attractive specialty of the game has become almost a lost art. No longer are the training hours devoted to a practice of "leads" or "breaks" or "slides." Several players on practically every club exceeded in individual stolen bases more than an entire club steals today. The hit and run, a much-overused play even in Ruth's day, as it is even now, likewise but not so unfortunately is more generally found on the shelf.

IN 1912, fifteen years before Ruth's home-run year of 1927, the American League record is 1,810 stolen bases—the peak year for the American League. In 1950, the nadir year for stolen bases by the American League, the record is 278.

In the twenty-five years preceding 1927, Ruth's home-run year, the American League had 30,511 stolen bases.

In the twenty-five years succeeding 1927, the American League had 12,537 stolen bases.

To conclude that the power hitting of Ruth was alone responsible for this almost incredible difference is certainly not true, and to determine accurately the exact part Ruth did play in reduced stolen bases brings one to the imponderables. The nonenforcement of the balk rule for many recent years had an effect, of course, on the diminishing stolen-base record, but the cheapness of a single added stolen base against the riches of a home-run clearance leaves the Ruthian influence almost untouched.

There is, today, a new generation of batsmen futilely trying to imitate Ruth. Weaklings and puny hitters now stroke for the fence. Ruth thus changed the whole objective of batting. From boyhood, the neophyte, the youth of our country indeed, tends to swing up to get a trajectory of great height. The Willie Keelers of the game are no more. It is all but disgraceful to be known as a "single hitter." A very prominent contemporary slugger in the National League very recently in a clubhouse speech told his locker mate, "Home runs are what they pay you for; nothing else counts."

It will not be surprising, unless some attention is given to the resiliency of the present baseball, if a number of major-league batsmen exceed the sixty mark within the next few years.

The Lajoies, the Delahantys, the Hornsbys, the Speakers, the Wagners, the DiMaggios, the Williamses, the Foxxes, the Greenbergs were power hitters in *size*, in stance, in wrist movement and bat sweep, equal in all respects to the present galaxy of home-run devotees—and they were all without covetousness; they would not have cared to compare themselves with the power of Ruth. Home Run Baker shared the lead in home runs with Sam Crawford in 1914 in the American League with eight home runs. No player in the A.L. for many years exceeded twenty. How come batsmen in the American League in 1961 hit 1,534 home runs, and an almost unknown with a batting percentage of .269 hit fifty-nine home runs in 154 games? The boy referred to, Maris, is a splendid power hitter, and I believe him to be a very modest gentleman. It is not to his discredit to say that his power as a baseball batsman is not comparable to Ruth's.

The sacrifice hit since Ruth's performance in 1927 has become a department left pretty largely to pitchers. Managers are practically compelled to change tactics to fit the batter's adjustment to the park and the "long ball." Managers, generally, do not play for the narrow margin of a one-run lead. The objective of every inning is many runs. Ruth brought all this about.

Ruth changed the pitcher's pitching policy. Study the bases on balls now and formerly. The pitcher now has to pitch with constant intent to the hitter's so-called weakness. He prefers to walk the batsman rather than give him the homer pitch. The game's tactics have removed many of the attractive suspense situations.

The press generally features the home run in the daily reports, and commentators likewise give its importance emphatic notice. Neither the manager nor the writers are to be blamed for this almost compulsory attention to the home runs. The public is fairly educated to demand the home run and seems to think, possibly correctly, that the excessive home runs are good for the game's gate. To me this is a regrettable circumstance only to be changed when and if the home runs become so excessive that power alone may be the only considered qualification in the selection of major-league players.

If one person's contribution can change the game as Ruth has understandably done, then no one can precede him in approaching baseball's pearly gates as an immortal.

Babe Ruth's grip shows his little finger off the handle of his famous 42-ounce bat.

Jackie Robinson

44

Jackie Robinson

IN THE SPRING of 1946 the unwritten rule that Negroes could not play in the major leagues was defied. It had been upheld for over half a century. Jackie Robinson broke the color line in baseball. Today there are approximately a hundred Negro players on the rosters of the two major leagues. Not only has baseball felt the impact of the Negro player, but the national problem of civil rights has been considerably affected by it. I believed that the first Negro in professional baseball should have a strong feeling about civil rights because such a person would have a comprehension of the race problem. He could not be the right person and feel only a personal problem. "If I am treated right, nothing else matters" could and would be the complete disqualification of the candidate. He would play a game of personal salvation and let it end there.

It was never in anyone's mind that a competent Negro player could not be found. There were plenty of them. No doubt about that, and very soon Brooklyn, having several Negro players, went out of its way to see to it that Larry Doby, a fine major-leaguer, went to Cleveland. Brooklyn needed a partner to develop the progress of Negro employment.

Brooklyn later sold the contract of its fifth colored major-league player, Samuel Jethroe, to Boston. Ownership thought there was a surfeit of colored boys on the Brooklyn club. The only reason for public acceptance of bringing in a Negro was to win a pennant. If then a fifth one would tend to lose a pennant, the reason for hiring Robinson was the identical reason for not hiring Jethroe.

The first major problem in breaking the color line was ownership. In St. Louis in 1942 and even later, a Negro was not permitted as a paid spectator to sit in the grandstand.

The ownership of Brooklyn at the first meeting in New York approved Negro employment. That was a new day for ownership in professional baseball, and George V. McLaughlin, James Mulvey, and Joe Gillideau (the board of directors of the Brooklyn Baseball Club) were heartily in favor.

There were many other problems. The last one—acceptance by Jackie's colleagues—could not be approached in advance, and the intervening four took two and a half years for final decision.

Robinson was signed to a Montreal contract, a subsidiary AAA club owned by Brooklyn. After his tremendous year at Montreal, in 1945, it became apparent that Jackie was something more than a possibility for the Brooklyn club. A peti-

tion was written and signed by a number of the players requesting his nonemployment. It took considerable effort and time and many personal conferences to remove this group opposition. Several boys wished to be traded to other clubs, and the captain of the team wrote a letter requesting his transfer.

THEN CAME that memorable game in Brooklyn, when with Robinson at bat the most abusive vilification from the opposition was rampant, and the entire Brooklyn club, led by Dixie Walker, Eddie Stanky, and Bobby Bragan—all three Southern boys with so-called Southern beliefs—protested with vigorous voice and challenge. From that moment on, Robinson felt that he had friends all about him. He belonged. That incident built a surprising fight and stick-to-itiveness in team morale that lifted the club from that time into pennant contention. The picture of Pee Wee Reese with his arm around Robinson's shoulders was greatly helpful as it appeared in the newspapers throughout the country.

One of the most worrying of all problems was finding the man who would be all right off the field. We could know about his playing ability in uniform—but what about out of uniform? Could he take it? What about his habits, his associates, his character, his education, his intelligence? Could the man handle his own people? Could he handle himself? What about transportation, hotels? What about the Jim Crow customs? Could he be fully and wisely cooperative in avoiding race adulation—gifts, dinners, awards, etc.? How could he oppose mass or group attendances of his own race?

How could a man of worth and human dignity bend enough? How could a man with a distinctive personality keep it untarnished with constant absorption of attacks calculated to destroy his self-respect? There just are not very many such humans. The trial candidate must never lose his sense of purpose nor lower his sights from the ultimate goal of making good off the field.

I had employed scouts in Puerto Rico, Cuba, and Mexico for over a year, only finally to find out that the best Negro players were in our own United States. One of the names on the list was Jackie Robinson. The scouting of the player was begun by Wendell Smith, a Negro writer for the Pittsburgh *Courier*. Then Wid Mathews followed up on him, followed by George Sisler and finally by Clyde Sukeforth. All these men believed they were scouting for the Brooklyn Brown Dodgers. Other than the reports of these very able experts, I knew nothing about the Negro player who was recommended. I simply accepted the judgment of my scouts.

Here was a boy who lacked a few hours' credit to a degree from UCLA. He had been a fine football player and a basketball and track star—less known in baseball than in any other major sport. He enlisted in the U.S. armed services as a private. He came out an officer. If direction determines value, Robinson was on his way.

Clyde Sukeforth brought Jackie to Brooklyn for an interview. This was the first time I had ever met him. Both Sukeforth and Robinson believed that he was to be offered a contract with the Brooklyn Brown Dodgers, a colored team. It was hard to convince the player that he was facing a job in the major leagues. At the end of a three-hour conference, Robinson showed the necessary intelligence and the strength of personality, but he had more and deeper racial resentment than was hoped for or expected. I tested and probed with many questions. If he were subjected to the very lowest depth of scurrility involving him and his own mother—"What would you do?"

"I'd kill him" showed the exact strength that was needed. But how could I bandage it and keep it fully alive?

AT THIS POINT, we spent several minutes reading a chapter on nonresistance from the book *The Life of Christ* by the great Italian priest Giovanni Papini, published in English about 1920. I just happened to have it handy in the top drawer of my desk. I thought it might become useful in the conference with Jackie.

"Ye have heard that it hath been said, An eye for an eye, and a tooth for a tooth: But I say unto you, That ye resist not evil: But whosoever shall smite thee on the right cheek, turn to him the other also. . . ." For an infinite number of believers this principle of not resisting evil has been the unendurable and inacceptable scandal of Christianity. There are three answers which men can make to violence: revenge, flight, turning the other cheek. The first is the barbarous principle of retaliation. . . . Flight is no better than retaliation. . . . The man who takes flight invites pursuit. . . . His weakness becomes the accomplice of the ferocity of others. . . . Turning the other cheek means not receiving the second blow. It means cutting the chain of the inevitable wrongs at the first link. Your adversary is ready for anything but this. . . . Every man has an obscure respect for courage in others, especially if it is moral courage, the rarest and most difficult sort of bravery. . . . It makes the very brute understand that this man is more than a man. . . . Man is a fighting animal; but with no resistance offered, the pleasure disappears; there is no zest left. . . . And yet the results of nonresistance, even if they are not always perfect, are certainly superior to those of resistance or flight. . . . To answer blows with blows, evil deeds with evil deeds, is to meet the attacker on his own ground, to proclaim oneself as low as he. . . . Only he who has conquered himself can conquer his enemies.

This was, by far, the most important point in the hiring of a Negro by a major-league club. Jackie Robinson is Christian by inheritance and practice. Well before the interview ended, he was fully convinced that the Papini doctrine was necessary and acceptable. He understood that the success of Negro employment in baseball depended very largely on himself.

This shocking move required, of course, some Booker T. Washington compromises with surface inequality for the sake of expediency. It would require constant and completely silent reaction to abuse—oral or physical. There could be but one direction of dedication—the doctrine of turning the other cheek. *There* came in the greatness of Jackie Robinson. "Punch for punch" was, by inheritance, by experience, and by desire, Jackie's quick and natural reaction to insult or attack. To self-impose control of every decent reflex was almost too much to ask for from any man, and particularly from Jackie. He was anything (one would think) but ideal for this "experiment." It took an intelligent man to understand the challenge—it took a man of great moral courage to accept it and see it through. He was both.

FOR THREE YEARS (that was the agreement) this boy was to turn the other cheek. He did, day after day, until he had no other to turn. They were both beat off. There were slight slip-ups on occasion in that first year in Montreal, that great city where all human beings are equal by nature regardless of their nationality or genesis.

Righteous impulse caught him unaware a couple of times, but Montreal was a great proving ground for the two years that followed. It took a few consultations and inspection tours. No one knows the trials and tribulations of Robinson during those three years. Jackie's wife, Rachel, knows most about them. That woman reminds one of Charles Lamb's description of the Negro—"those images of God cut in ebony." She is a graduate of the University of California at Los Angeles, with a refinement of culture that should grace every graduate of a great university. She was Jackie's tower to lean on and constant guidepost too. She was a great help.

So the first contribution of Jackie Robinson—so well known to Rachel and a few others—that qualified him for greatness was the self-imposed restraint to preserve and advance healthy race relations under terrifically trying circumstances. In 1949, Paul Robeson, the famous actor and singer, hit the public press, stating, in part, that in event of war between the Soviet Union and the United States, the Negroes of our country would not join the military forces. Jackie was then asked to testify before the House Committee on Un-American Activities to answer Robeson. "And white people must realize," said Jackie, "that the more a Negro hates Communism because it opposes democracy, the more he is going to hate any other influence that kills off democracy in this country—and that goes for racial discrimination in the Army, and segregation on trains and buses, and job discrimination because of religious beliefs or color or place of birth."

Robinson made other remarks that day in our nation's capital that showed the fire of his patriotism. I liked the closing sentence in his testimony: "We can win our fight without the Communists and we don't want their help."

His Americanism is very genuine and enduring. Negro citizens of America should not attempt to bask in the reflected glory of one Negro's achievement. Jackie needs no hero worship by his people. He does not regard himself as a hero. He asks for nothing from anyone other than an equal chance for all our people for jobs, for education, for a place to live, to go, to come, to speak, to be as one pleases within decency and the law. And Negro Americans should feel and show only quiet gratitude for the load this fellow citizen carried for their sake.

There never has been a man in the game who could put mind and muscle together quicker and with better judgment than Robinson. No one could be heard to find serious fault if Robinson were given the second-base position on the all-time All-American club. He was not as great a right-hand batsman as Rogers Hornsby. No one was—not even Wagner or Jim Delahanty or Lajoie. But he was a skillful batsman with good power. He was a play maker—right or left. He could start and/or finish the double play par excellence. He was a fastidious roamer on fly balls—fair or foul—all over. With a call of two strikes, no man living, then or now, could threaten a pitcher with more imminent disaster. On the base paths he could turn a ball game around. He was a student of pitchers' moves and an instant learner of them—a master of commanding leads and making the daring "break."

This man was a judge of players, all players, yours and the other fellow's. Well do I remember a conversation with Jackie a day or so after he had first faced a young pitcher on the Pittsburgh club. Purkey was his name.

"Mr. Rickey, you have one young pitcher who can be very good. It's tough to get the middles together." (He meant the bat and the ball middles.) How right he was, at a time when Purkey had no rating anywhere. Jackie's alacrity and correctness in cataloguing players and teams marked him high for managerial timber. And he is just that. Give him complete control of emotion and I know of no one better qualified for major-league management.

The Baseball Writers of America elected him to the Hall of Fame on merit. It is unfair to them and without due honor to Robinson to say that the vote was determined by color.

ONLY Cobb and very few others carried the disturbing badge of fear all the time he wore a uniform. There was concealed explosion in the relaxed and indifferent walk as Robinson shuffled along after the play was over. Don't be fooled by it. He was hard to beat. If he had entered the big leagues many years sooner (as he should have), the record books would need alteration in many directions.

In 1944, Dr. Edmund Raymond Soper wrote a book titled *Racism*. Dr. Soper had been born in Tokyo, Japan, and was a university professor of comparative religions, an educator of considerable note. Two years later, Robinson met Dr. Soper and came to appreciate Dr. Soper's thinking on the subject of racism.

In this book I find this prophetic sentence, written twenty years ago: "Of all the ills to which humanity finds itself heir today, there is none more virulent and none which has so many facets, involves so many world issues, as that of race."

The development and history of these past twenty years would certainly permit Dr. Soper to write this sentence again without change. *On May 4, 1963, the front page of the New York Times showed a picture of Negroes being hosed in Birmingham, Alabama, while the sports page reported a Negro ballplayer from Birmingham being honored in New York.* But he would say again, as he often did, that Jackie Robinson has contributed to the alleviation of the ill of racism. And Jackie, now retired from the playing field, quietly says that the "challenge to baseball and to all our people, white or black, is to believe that Dr. Soper states the truth—and to act upon it."

All-Time Team

FOR ALL OF US who have played baseball as boys and have had the good fortune to play it professionally as men and then remain in the game as coaches or managers or club officials, excellence of play is unforgettable. The outstanding players can be judged and matched quite accurately in baseball, because so many games are played on the successive days of a season. Comparisons can be made in the excellence of play at each position, and the various qualities of players are memorized by every fan. The intangibles, such as desire and courage and mental quickness, take longer to discover, but over the years, these too come forth and can be measured.

Perhaps we have all secretly picked our all-star teams at one time or another, year after year. We select our team on reputation or on record or on limited observation. In our imagination we think of the incredible game these titans would play if they were all together on one diamond.

I've thought a great deal about my own All-Time Team. It has been a preposterous undertaking to choose thirty players from the major-league rosters of the past seventy-five years. There is that closeness in ability that leaves me unwilling to debate with you that your choice is not better than mine. With the exception of one of the thirty players I have named, I have been acquainted with all of them and have observed them closely, both on and off the field, over the years.

Baseball over a hundred years has furnished greatness to many more than double the thirty. I quickly concede the right of critics to choose a different team. It just happens that I know better the men I have selected.

There are five player departments in baseball: catching, first base, infield, outfield, and pitching. I will discuss my selections in that order.

Catching

MY THREE CATCHERS on this squad would be first off: Mickey Cochrane, then Roy Campanella and Bill Delancey.

Of the three catchers, I believe the first choice should be Cochrane for several reasons. In the sixty years of my acquaintanceship with catchers, I don't know one who could outrun him. Except Lou Criger and Hack Spencer and possibly Jimmy Archer, there has been no catcher I know of who could outthrow him, and for both hitting average and power, Cochrane was superb. He was a take-charge guy. He had baseball sense and managerial sense, too. He was the manager of Detroit for several years.

The second catcher is Roy Campanella. He would have had many more years left to play if he had not been seriously injured in an automobile accident. He was a consistent power hitter, feared by every club, and he was a perfect receiver. Baseball managers called him a "smart onion," always in command. His arm was strong and accurate, and he took charge of his pitchers. He assumed authority. He was a quick and accurate judge of any young pitcher and would confidently predict his future.

MANY PEOPLE don't know very much about Delancey. He was tubercular. "Quick consumption," they called it. He played only one year, really. As a kid, he took the catching job away from the first-string catcher on the champion Cardinal club in 1934. Got into the seven-game World Series that year and caught every inning. He was the most hardened practical joker in baseball that I ever knew, worse than Johnnie Evers. He had an originality in planning ridiculous situations. He was the worst one of the Gashouse Gang as a designing manipulator of incongruities. On the field he knew everything. He knew the movements of base runners backwards and forwards and learned the hitting traits of batsmen overnight. He anticipated managerial tactics and acted on his judgment. He had remarkable pitching sense. He was, too, an effective psychologist. He knew how to talk to a batter—and when to do it or not to do it. He was a master with his pitchers, old or young, and the pitchers knew it. He knew there's a lingering hold on the consciousness of the last pitch that hasn't passed by yet with the hitter. He's still seeing it, he's still thinking about it. It may be that you should throw that next pitch within five seconds. That was Delancey's thinking.

Delancey knew the time to delay an anxious power hitter who could hardly wait for the next pitch. Let him exercise, let him exercise a lot. That's what Grover Alexander told me when he struck out Lazzeri in the 1926 World Series. Lazzeri was just crazy to hit, swinging three bats vigorously as Alexander was coming from the bull pen. So Alexander got all ready and then he went to the resin bag, got ready again, and then stepped back and got some more resin. Shook his head a couple of times at the catcher's signal. He thought Lazzeri had worn himself out. Alexander told me that Lazzeri was struck out before he pitched a ball. Now that was not Delancey, but Delancey was great at that kind of ham acting, at studying the psychology of every situation. It was subconsciously a part of him. He was a natural student of what, how, and when. *And he could hit! And throw! And run!* He was unafraid physically and morally. He was a hell raiser, but he was victory bound.

First Base

FIFTY YEARS AGO, I knew that you had to have two first basemen. First base is a distinctive department of the club's personnel —as much as the outfield or infield or catching. A substitute in any other department may not be able to play first base.

My choice of the two first basemen are George Sisler and Lou Gehrig. I have given my analysis of George Sisler's qualifications in the preceding section on the immortals. The ability and character and personality of Lou Gehrig combine splendidly to make him a national hero. However, he makes the All-Time Team because he could hit and run and field. Only Sisler could rate him.

Infield

LIMITED AS I AM to thirty players, only six infielders can be included. I will now give you the six infielders in alphabetical order:
Edward Trowbridge Collins—slim, long legs, split to the navel. He could run as fast as Sisler and could slide as elusively as Cobb or George Watkins. Twenty-five years in a major-league uniform, he stole 743 bases. The balk rule was enforced and he had a decent chance. He played 2,826 games, almost all of them at second base. He lacked 51 AB's of coming to bat 10,000 times, and every third time he made a base hit. He was among the top line-drive hitters of all time.

He qualified in every man's definition of a gentleman from Socrates to Herbert Hoover. Cobb chose him first of all as the All-Time second baseman and would ride roughshod over anyone who disputed him. I could not sleep comfortably if I left him off my team.

I want Frank Frisch as one of my infielders because he could play third, second, or shortstop as

a first-choice regular. He could hit and field and was a base runner and a base stealer. Frisch had a great responsiveness to the tension game. "This is it!" He was a money player.

Frisch joins Collins and Sisler in the trio of baseball's academic intellectuals. Neither Columbia nor Michigan propelled the student habit down the years in Collins and Sisler to the extent that Fordham did in Frisch. Frank has extended his cultural interests from horticulture to broadcasting, and his restive spirit found passing satisfaction in playing baseball—for years, for money. He benefited every employer.

Rogers Hornsby. The most overlooked quality of Hornsby's excellence was his running speed. His reputation rests largely on the universal acceptance of his hitting ability; he was the greatest right-hand batter of all time, better than Delahanty or Lajoie. He could outrun the dash man on the track team of two great universities—and he did. Hornsby did not enjoy sliding, but he never failed to slide when it was needed. Neither did he like the fly ball in back of him.

He had hitting form personified. The pedagogical flag he carried bore the inscription "Look at me and do your best." As a player he seldom had a word of instruction for anyone or a suggestion for the rookie.

Physical excellence was his constant possession. He would not go to picture shows. "It will not help my eyes," he said to me. His weight was important down to the very ounce. He had more batting ego than Sisler or Cobb. He knew and he knew he knew. I don't think he ever had a slump. He was full of unspoken sorrow for the pitcher. "He doesn't amount to a row of pins," he said to me in reply to my complimentary remark about the pitcher who had just struck him out. Surely he was the greatest pinch hitter of all time, and he was equal to Jackie Robinson when the call was two strikes.

Among the six is Jackie Robinson. He was second only to Honus Wagner in defensive versatility. I put him ahead of Frisch in this respect. He could play any position, and I mean just that. He could pitch or catch with instant aptitude. Jackie Robinson came the nearest to Cobb in the field of adventure, chance taking, and, if anything, Robinson "adventured" with better judgment. Cobb took more chances, but Robinson had a better percentage of probabilities. Cobb played professionally at seventeen, but due to the war, Robinson started at twenty-six. His versatility is proven by the record. Originally a shortstop, then a great major-league first baseman, without previous practice, he played most years at second and ended up at third. With two strikes, I know of no batsman to excel him. He was just as abandoned

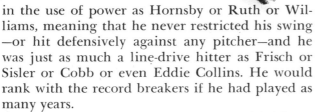

Joe DiMaggio
The most beloved great player in modern baseball.

in the use of power as Hornsby or Ruth or Williams, meaning that he never restricted his swing —or hit defensively against any pitcher—and he was just as much a line-drive hitter as Frisch or Sisler or Cobb or even Eddie Collins. He would rank with the record breakers if he had played as many years.

Pie Traynor played 1,864 games at third base, leading the National League for all time, and no one could become seriously unpopular in western Pennsylvania if he were to choose Pie to start the All-Time game as the third baseman. Many regard him the most nearly perfect defensively of all third basemen. With a great arm, great hands,

great body control, quickness and speed, and disposition, he was an ideal team man; he fits in any group. He could hit for distance—and he could run. A hard man to double. Pie Traynor belongs.

At shortstop there is only one, Honus Wagner. He has to be the man because there is nobody equal to him. I have discussed Wagner at length as one of my immortals.

It is with deep personal regret that I have not included Charles Gehringer. He was a great second baseman and a great hitter. But when I extend the list, more great players come to mind and my regrets multiply.

The Outfield

O F THE SEVEN outfielders on my All-Time Team, the three greatest are Cobb, Ruth, and Joe Jackson. Cobb and Ruth I have already discussed. The controversial Joe Jackson could run, throw, and field, and if God ever permitted birth to a natural hitter, it was Jackson. Many batsmen of his day would join me in saying that. Cobb said it often and right out loud.

It will be said here and there that to include Jackson makes me indifferent to the integrity of the game. I wish to say a word about that anticipated criticism. Joe Jackson was blacklisted for cooperative knowledge of a fix. If there is "a wideness in God's mercy like the wideness of the sea," then there must be a "kindness in His justice" that permits redemption to Joe Jackson. He suffered a lifetime of penance for his ignorant acquiescence. I know about it and I make no apologies to anyone for including Joe Jackson on the All-Time Team. Jackson was the star player in the "Black Sox" World Series games of 1919. The fact that "a false good became a true evil" in Jackson's case in no respect affects the integrity of professional baseball.

My four other outfielders are Tris Speaker, Joe DiMaggio, Ted Williams, and Stanley Musial. If I had to choose them in order, Joe DiMaggio would not be last.

Stanley Musial is the people's choice for a place on the All-Time All-Star Team. His retirement as a player brought about universal attention, and baseball people—from the Commissioner on down through all the professional clubs—gave more lavish tribute to Stanley than was accorded any other

player in the history of the game, including Babe Ruth. His playing justified all the honors that have come to him, but the public liked him because of his great contribution off the field. Stanley Musial is a participating citizen in his community, and his sterling qualities as a gentleman are firmly nailed on the billboards of fame for endless posterity. For twenty-two years he was first on the field and last off it. He played in 3,026 games and made more hits than any other player in the game. He has broken about fifty individual statistical records, most of which will never be equaled or approached.

He was technically as scientific a hitter as Cobb, had a good arm and good speed, and was a fearless fielder.

In the country graveyard where I shall be buried, it would be an acceptable epitaph on the modest marker of the same size as my dear relatives thereabouts if it were to read:

> He had something to do with
> changing Stanley Musial from
> a pitcher to an outfielder.

That would give me transient distinction for my nineteen grandchildren.

When Ted Williams is included on the All-Time roster, everyone should keep in mind his three years of enforced military service in the Marine Air Corps. These three years were chopped out at the peak of his record making—when Ted was twenty-three, and twenty-four, and twenty-five years of age. Then he was called back to military service in 1952, with wide public sym-

Stan Musial

The Man represents all that is good in baseball
and combined the qualities of the
old-time ball player and the modern star.

52

ROBERT RIGER

pathy and considerable disapproval. He played only six games that season. He got back a year later, in 1953, in time to play in thirty-seven games. In other words, he missed five years in the service of his country, and no one anywhere ever heard him or his family murmur a word of complaint. In fact, at that time, Ted said publicly that he was pleased to be able to serve. No other professional baseball player ever experienced superimposed career impairment equal to Ted Williams'. His baseball salary at that time was said to be $90,000.

It is reasonable to believe that Ted would have made many book records in power hitting if his major-league play had been continuous. He rates with Ruth in the flexibility of his wrists, enabling him to hit at the last part of a second and reach the bleachers.

Tris Speaker. If Jackson were to be moved out of the front row, I would be one of a large majority who would vote for Tris Speaker along with Cobb and Ruth. He covered more ground in position play in the pre-pitch than any center fielder I ever knew. Much has been written about his great fielding ability. He was noted for playing close to the infield. He was unexcelled in going back for the fly ball. He prided himself on his generally successful effort to catch every fly ball in body position to throw it instantly. If I were choosing an outfielder on the basis of fielding alone, I would take Speaker. He played almost 2,800 games in center field for Boston and Cleveland, and the record shows that he averaged thirty stolen bases for each full season. For a period of twenty consecutive years, an admiring American public would laugh its sides out with jocular derision if he were not playing center field on the American League all-star team. He hit .344 as a lifetime average, and his power was always close to the top. He came from Texas, but he made many friends everywhere. He really did, and I mean friends. He was a beloved player.

This completes the list of outfielders permitted on a thirty-player-limit All-Time Team.

However, my sleep has been disturbed in recent days because I have not included a very great player who could make any All-Time line-up probably at any position—pitching, catching, or first base, and I could imagine him the nearest thing to Honus Wagner as a shortstop of anybody I know. He plays in the outfield. While I have not named him as one of the outfielders, I am sure that every one of the seven outfielders I have selected would be pleased to have me give honorable mention to Willie Mays.

I believe that any grandstander who knows his baseball will not disagree on this selection for honorable mention if he will watch Mays and only Mays, both offensively and defensively, in any nine-inning game. This means, for example, that you do not see the pitcher deliver a single pitch nor a single batter swing at a ball, nor do you follow the course of any fly ball to the infield or outfield, but instead you see only Mays. Then you will agree. I challenge any baseball man to observe Mays in uniform on offense and defense for 7,200 consecutive seconds and, with a clear conscience, not include mention of him on the All-Time Team.

This fellow plays the game *all* the time.

His hitting, fielding, throwing, running, discipline, health, agility, and desire rate him with the best. In modern baseball, Mays is in a class by himself

Pitching

Now follows my All-Time roster of twelve pitchers:

I start with the oldest, the remarkable Cy Young. There's an encouraging word about Cy Young for the young pitchers of today. A giant in stature, he was probably the wildest youngster that ever came to fame as a great pitcher. It is likely that his pitching records in his first days in the minor leagues of professional baseball set the high mark for bases on balls. But he became a great strike-out king with control. He won 511 games in his major-league career. That's a world record.

Charles "Kid" Nichols is selected on reputation and particularly on his record. He had six out of seven consecutive seasons in one span when he won thirty games or more. The book does not reveal a comparable record. I never saw Nichols pitch. His last season in the National League was 1905, the same year I signed with Mr. McAleer of the St. Louis Browns. I came to know Kid Nichols very well in later years, and when he was presented at Cooperstown to the Hall of Fame, I had the honor of speaking on that occasion about his many deserving qualifications. I doubt if there is any other pitcher in the Hall of Fame of his diminutive size. When I visited with him at Cooperstown in 1945, he told me that his pitching weight in his heyday was 145 pounds. He was undoubtedly the greatest pitcher of like poundage, but there were several great pitchers who pitched in the major leagues at 150 pounds or under. I recognize Nichols out of respect for the judgment of men like John McGraw and Wilbert Robinson and others of their time and type who regarded Nichols as the best in his day.

Surely no one will disagree with including on

Rube Waddell

The Philadelphia southpaw
died young but won about
197 games and had a wild
time on and off the diamond.

my All-Time pitching staff Connie Mack's Rube Waddell. In a little over eleven seasons he struck out 2,310 batters. Waddell was something, the way he would give you that ridiculous windup—moving his arms all over the sky and then bringing the ball to a practical stop at his belt and—*wham!* —all the windup had nothing to do with the pitch. It started from the belt. When he had control—and some sleep—he was unbeatable. You were just a defensive batsman up there.

Now Addie Joss, a Cleveland pitcher of sixty years ago, is one of the twelve. His career was comparatively short, but anyone who saw him or played against him would not argue with me. If I were choosing an all-time team of gentlemen from professional baseball, Addie Joss would be the captain. He was universally beloved, as was Walter Johnson, but he had a more assertive personality than Walter. Well do I remember the day in Cleveland when I had finished the pre-game practice. I turned about and there was Addie Joss with a fungo bat in his hand ready to hit to the outfield. He said to me, "Branch, you throw too much. Everyone knows you have a fine arm, but you overuse it, and you will make more money throughout the years if you keep your arm. Don't hurt it."

I was greatly pleased to have voluntary counsel from an even then famous pitcher. And I said to him, "Yes, thank you, but I'm catching more games than the other two catchers put together and I'm the lowest-paid of the three."

He grabbed my shirtfront and sternly said, "Don't you ever let me hear you say that again." Then slowly and deliberately he continued, "Make yourself needed and you will be paid." Then he dropped his hand and walked away. For the next fifty-seven years his counsel has helped me. However, it is not because of his gentlemanliness that I include Addie Joss. Not at all. He was truly one of the greatest pitchers in my acquaintance. His record supports my choice.

Of all the pitchers that I've ever known or known about, Christy Mathewson comes first. He had everything, he was everything, and he did everything. He is the only pitcher I have included as an immortal.

Of all the knuckle-ballers, including Eddie Rommell, Jess Haines, Burleigh Grimes, Al Orth and a few others, surely Ed Walsh of the early-century Chicago White Sox comes first. As home-run hitters are known for their power, Walsh is known for his force. He was a power-full man. His knuckle ball was fast—faster than Orth's. He had speed on his knuckle ball that no other man ever had, and it seemed that he could throw the ball harder in the ninth inning than he would in the first. In his day, American League managers would undoubtedly have voted him the leading pitcher of the league. In 1908 he won forty games and lost fifteen. Those were the days of my acquaintance with him.

Walter Johnson of the Washington Club would be on everyone's all-time team. I've often heard baseball men compare Johnson with Mathewson. The one had a great head and a good arm; the other had a great arm and a good head. One with a great assortment of pitches, the other with one pitch.

But it's like saying what would Paderewski do for a living if he couldn't play the piano. He *could*

54

play the piano. Johnson *could* throw a fast ball. He didn't need anything else. That's all there was to it. He won 416 games. I do not want to leave the impression that Walter Johnson didn't have a curve ball. He did have a fairly good curve ball, but he used it comparatively seldom. He set the all-time record for strike-outs at 3,508. He also leads in shutouts with 113, lifetime. It is fantastic conjecture to imagine what Johnson would have done on a first-division team.

Grover Cleveland Alexander. The imperturbable. His World Series performance against Tony Lazzeri in 1926 was no surprise to Manager Hornsby or to anyone else who knew "Old Pete." A great pitcher in the pinch. A Nebraska country boy, second only to Mathewson as a control pitcher and second to none with his repertoire of effective pitches. He holds the all-time record for shutouts in one season: sixteen. In five of six years (1915 to 1920) he led the National League in earned run average.

When he was past forty years of age in 1927, Alexander won twenty-one games for the St. Louis Cardinals. He was a kindly, well-intentioned individual. Twice he took the Narcosan treatment for alcoholism. He deserved the sympathy and understanding of players, managers, owners, writers, and the public generally, for he so sincerely wanted to quit drinking.

Walking about restlessly in my room in the Auditorium Hotel in Chicago in 1927, grasping an imaginary bottle against his chest, with the tears streaming down his face, he said to me, "When I take a drink, it just seems I can't let it go. I keep on and take it all." A few days later, he took his second Narcosan treatment.

I never knew him to have an enemy—only one, himself.

Carl Hubbell was probably greatest among that class of pitchers who continually present the problem of timing. He was a "change of speed" pitcher. He produced perfect deception with varying velocities and deflections because his angle and dexterity of delivery were identical on all pitches. He did not really have great speed, but there was ever the illusion of the fast ball because of the contrasting changes. His record shows forty-six and a third consecutive shutout innings and twenty-four consecutive victories. What an incredible edge this is to a club going for a flag!

Dizzy Dean was hardly a jump below a demon on the mound. I could tell you stories on how he came through on so many special occasions. He was just about as good as he wanted to be. Every pitch was *it*—and he inherited physical stature and endurance. About all the scoring ever done off Dean in his heyday would be due to his jocularity, his carelessness, his momentary indifference, his

babying along, knowing he "had them beat." On occasion he'd be an experimental pitcher. He could throw everything in the book. He would see an opposing pitcher throwing a knuckle ball or this or that kind of a pitch and within a day or so he could beat the other fellow at his own specialty. While he could throw everything from all angles of delivery, when the game was on he would usually confine himself to one delivery and three pitches—most of the time two pitches: a curve and a fast ball. He had unforgettable ego, but he deserves not to be forgotten.

Bob Feller had speed almost equal to Walter Johnson's. He had a usable unusual curve and he employed it. Like Ted Williams, he carved out of the very center of his baseball life critical years spent in the military service. I must use the word once more. He was *great*.

Then there is the youngest of the twelve—Warren Spahn, the most debatable selection that has confronted me. I have studied the records of Ford, Grove, Koufax, and Plank—all left-handers —and several other great pitchers, both left and right. I know them all and I can compare Spahn with every one of them. Perhaps I chose Spahn because I know more about him. I have seen him pitch more than any of the others and I may be guilty of personal bias. I think not. Plank was a personal friend, and I have profound admiration for Whitey Ford both on and off the field. I have known Lefty Grove since he started, and I tried to sign Sandy Koufax to a Pittsburgh contract shortly after he graduated from high school.

Spahn is a student of batsmen and a perfectionist in his repertoire of pitches. I am not apologetic to anyone for including Spahn on the All-Time pitching staff. Finally, Spahn has won twenty games or more thirteen times, and as I write this he has won sixty-one percent of his games to date. And he is not through!

M Y GUIDING RULE in the selection of this team, once again, is the courage that instinctive play requires. I'd rather have one man willing to embrace the rational hazards of chance than a whole field full of know-it-alls who do nothing. At a time of great national debate in the French assembly, Anatole France stated it better than I have when he said, "I prefer the errors of enthusiasm to the indifference of wisdom."

Well, there is my team—the thirty men. Twelve of them are still living; only one is active. By and large they are gentlemen of good sportsmanship, exemplary character, and great desire.

A Boy, a Bat and a Ball

Babe Ruth said during his last visit to Yankee Stadium, when his voice was almost gone, "Start him when he's young, teach him to play baseball when he's four years old...."

With a bat and a ball and his imagination a boy is a complete team. He can swing at the ball, chop at it, golf at it. He can run after it, use the trees for bases, or throw the ball against the side of the house and learn to catch it. This is how the game begins, how the boy discovers it. To hit a ball, to throw it, to catch it are exhilarating successes that he attempts again and again. It is a morning in early May and there is the four-year-old boy running along a shaded sidewalk in Nashua, New Hampshire. It is the same in Birmingham, Alabama, or Lubbock, Texas, or San Jose, California. With a bat and a ball this young boy is *every boy*—and to his father at one time or another he

is, secretly, Babe Ruth in one generation, Ted Williams in another, Willie Mays today.

Baseball will always endure because it is played in the summer when the boys are home from school. Baseball is a romance that begins when a boy is very young. It starts him dreaming and teaches him to hope. It brings a diamond into his vision where the bases are fixed and the outfield is endless, and he begins to *care* about playing, about hitting the ball past everyone and rounding the bases, touching them and sliding home. He finds accomplishment in the diamond, something he can measure. It gives him direction and becomes a vital part of his summer.

Hitting a ball and scoring a run are in a way what all of us try to do all our lives. Baseball becomes a symbol, win or lose, and the romance never really ends.

The Vacant Lot

The apparently uncontrolled surge of moral delinquency in our great cities is more or less directly the result of misused leisure. Leisure is wonderful in creative hands. It accounts for great architecture, great paintings, and great music. People who can be masters of their own time have given us great literature and great artistic blessings of all kinds. Leisure, however, is a damnable thing in the hands of adolescent boyhood. I would rather see a boy with a broken leg on the field of play than one with a broken character in the recess of idleness—nothing to do.

A great American historian has said that it is just too bad that the history of nations could not have been written judging a people from their play at games rather than from their indulgence in wars.

If a great Senator from a great state can make an extended speech in the Senate on the unbridled criminality of teenagers in the Nation's capitol, and if a great philosopher and teacher, William James, can infer that competitive sport might properly direct the physical-combat instinct of youth, rather than the drill at arms, isn't it timely to suggest that the U.S. government could afford through the Department of Health, Education, and Welfare, to institute a plan of organized sport in all our cities, where former playgrounds have unfortunately been removed? Why, indeed, should youth diversion not have a Cabinet post of its own? It is significant that this great national game of baseball can remove monotony and idleness from the summer lives of 30,000,000 boys.

Boys will play baseball anywhere.

In the drab streets of the city their playing field has no fixed dimension. It is a side street where, between the sewer covers, they play stickball. Or curb ball; a rubber ball is bounced off the edge of the curbstone and caroms sharply in different directions around the infield. Or punch ball; the pitcher puts English on a one-bounce pitch and the hitter punches the ball with his fists (with time out for passing cars). It is the crowded school playgrounds where the outfielder is in the middle of a basketball game. Occasionally the boys of the city will find the wealth of new dirt on the site of a demolished building and will play with the lines of windows as their grandstand. In the smaller communities, baseball is played on the vacant lot.

We always had a ritual in the cities and in the country of "choosing up." In the hills of Pennsylvania or off a highway in Ohio or alongside a wheat field in Kansas, boys would have pickup games. All sizes and shapes would meet and choose up sides with a bat. There always seemed to be an odd number, so one would have to play for both sides.

Sometimes there would be only two outfielders and gloves would be borrowed. If a boy came around in a baseball uniform—something his aunt, who never came to see him very often, had sent him—he was out of place. Usually the kid with the uniform couldn't play well, and he'd always get picked last or not at all.

These casual meetings of the boys were fun, but they were haphazard. Also, after World War II, suburban and urban development were extensive, and the vacant lots began to disappear. What the young boys needed was practical guidance and leadership in playing the game. Most of all they needed to get away from the sand lot and the discouragement of broken glass, rocks, nearby windows and no backstops to a field with a diamond where they could really play baseball.

National Symbol

It seems for half the years of my life I saw the countryside flashing by from a train window or from a bus window rattling between small towns and cities everywhere to play baseball. Then suddenly the world changed. Now we are in the age of flight. Ball clubs fly across the entire United States to play a game in less time than the train would take from New York to Washington. From a plane window the landscape is etched everywhere with the baseball diamond. All across America it is stamped on the land. It is a national symbol—in the center of a housing project or the edge of a quiet residential community, in clusters in city parks or alone in an open field at the foot of a mountain in the West. It is always there, everywhere—*the American Diamond.*

The beginning came just after World War II. Suddenly there was a new idea from a small town in Pennsylvania, Williamsport, to add to the period of adjustment and beginning after the war a chance for organizing a baseball program for boys twelve years of age and under. Carl Stotz was the founder, and he called the game played on a smaller diamond Little League baseball. It was a neighborhood idea. It established the diamond for the boy at last. Parents and friends came to watch them play. There were tryouts. Every boy had a chance, and there were uniforms and good instruction. Little League was full of action and fun, and the diamonds spread across the land.

A Team, a League

Three teams comprised the first Little League in Williamsport. The next year it grew to four. In 1947 there were sixty teams and the United States Rubber Company subsidized the program and promoted it nationally. In 1948 there were 416 teams, in 1951 over 3,000, and in 1955, 16,000. In 1963 it had doubled to over 33,000 teams and 6,000 leagues in twenty-six nations, playing a quarter of a million games each season. Four million boys have played the game.

Each of the unit leagues has been grouped geographically into 400 districts with a volunteer district administrator to coordinate the Little League program in the area. The league is the basic unit of organization. It includes from four to eight teams. From twelve to fifteen players are selected for each team by means of a standard tryout system. Any boy who will be nine years old before August first and will not attain the age of 13 before that date each year is eligible to compete. A team of fifteen boys must have only seven twelve-year-olds, six eleven-year-olds, and at least two who are nine or ten. The boys are given good physical checkups, and they wear stout batting helmets that cover their ears. Boys who don't make it are accommodated in a farm system where their skills can be developed. Little did I know when I pioneered the farm system that someday it would include eight-year-olds.

Games are played after school in the spring about five-thirty in the afternoon between teams of the same league. No admission is ever charged. The games go six innings, and the umpires, managers, and coaches are adults who volunteer and enjoy working with children. Leadership is the most important single factor in the program. If a team manager loses one of his players through illness or injury or if the boy moves out of the neighborhood, he may obtain another player. The playing ability of any boy is not considered a justifiable reason for replacement.

At the end of the neighborhood season the teams in one league will pick an all-star team made up of the fourteen best boys who will play in tournament competition outside their league in broader geographical areas to decide a regional champion to go to Williamsport and play in the annual Little League World Series. Each regional winner (four from the United States and one each from Canada, Latin America, Europe, and the Pacific) qualifies to play in the Series. In recent years the teams return home after a visit to Washington, D.C., as a memorable parting adventure as Little Leaguers.

The First Battery

In Little League any player on a team's roster may pitch, but no more than five pitchers can be used in one game. For the safety of the boys, a Little League pitcher may not pitch more than six innings in a calendar week, and after having pitched four innings in a game he may not pitch again for three days. Only two pitchers on a team who are twelve years old may pitch in one week, so this gives the nine-year-old southpaw (*at left*) the chance he's been waiting for ever since he was a little kid. In the soft evening light of a Tuesday afternoon in late April he makes his first start. The uniform is baggy on his wispy frame, the ball is like a grapefruit in his hand, but he artfully conceals his pitch. Determined as a boy who really wants to win can be, he pitches two shutout innings! His catcher is cool and wise beyond his years. A crackerjack, pepperpot, sassy imp who can do everything behind the plate and knows it. The two boys complement each other. There is a unique bond of friendship in this first battery of pitcher and catcher in Little League that each will long remember.

The catcher is as big as the umpire—until the umpire stands up—so there's no sense in arguing a call. He just holds that mitt up there and makes a good target and yells, "Hum it to me, babe!"

The Perils of the Trade

There come early in the career of every Little League ballplayer the first lessons of failure and defeat. Losing! Adversity for a boy is tough to take, especially out there on his own. He learns the white line between fair and foul is narrow and luck goes both ways.

The photograph at right is a masterpiece, a tribute to the perils of the trade. The pitcher who has lost his control early in the game.

Number twelve is the second baseman. He's telling the shortstop he doesn't know why the other team's batters weren't swinging at those pitches, they were beautiful. "They don't know what's good," says the shortstop. The third baseman walks carefully one step to the rear of the pitcher and in a confident tone says, "Gee whiz, Charlie, don't feel so bad, it's only the first inning and you still got a no-hitter going. It's just those eleven bases on balls that gave 'em the lead they got. Remember, pal, we ain't even been up yet." The manager is coming out head down and thinking precisely how to put it to the boy that he just doesn't have it today (and later where he made his mistakes on his follow-through). The little catcher knows this is one of those days when Charlie has no stuff and figures he won't say anything unless they ask.

Charlie is burning. He tugs at his shirt sleeve. He's too disgusted and ashamed to speak, but his face under that cap portrays the eternal message of the pitcher who was wild!

Now follow the sequence below of the shortstop booting a grounder on a sure double-play ball. *1.* Ground ball slips off glove, hits off chest and shoots upwards. (The coach will tell him later he was holding his glove palm up instead of fingers up and palm away.) *2.* His eyes follow ground ball as it becomes fly ball. *3.* He springs after ball in eager pursuit, losing cap. *4.* Ball lands as runner goes by. *5.* On the pickup to throw the ball slips and drops. *6.* As he bends to pick it up, foot and fate kick ball away. *7.* Body becomes more frozen now, unlike picture 3, as boy realizes he is alone and there are noises from everywhere. *8.* Finally, help arrives from the second baseman who was waiting on the bag with the guy who hit the ball. It will be a long way to the dugout, and when the shortstop gets there the fellows will give him the needle. He will still be chasing that ball when he comes up to bat again, and that won't help either. Here's where the coach can help with a word. The fibers are strengthened right here.

The coaches and managers and umpires have an enormous responsibility, for they must realize that each boy is different, and even at the young age of a Little League player they must respect the individual personalities of the boys who want to be "big" in every way, want to grow up fast and to make it, *belong* to a group of boys. That is what a team is.

The men have to bring the boys along. They must enjoy baseball and help the boys gain satisfaction from how they play the game—win or lose. They must communicate the desire and enthusiasm of wanting to play well and wanting to win. By good example, the adults set the tone of the courage it takes to accept the breaks, the bitter disappointment of defeat, crushing as it may seem in the perspective of a ten-year-old boy. In achieving discipline, the coaches must mellow all of their teaching with a happy sense of humor.

1. *2.* *3.* *4.*

5.

6.

7.

8.

Practice and Skill

Out of the days of trial and error, of success and failure and of long hours of practice and effort, come the skills to play the game. For some, skill comes quickly and surely, to others only after discouraging mistakes, to others not at all. Most boys have a flair for baseball and the skill comes—with practice and knowledge. Style is confidence. And the Little League ballplayer's confidence has grown over three years with sound instruction and the patience of five coaches and managers. These are pictures of twelve-year-old boys who *know* they can make the play.

One other factor has helped his development and is directly related to the successful growth of Little League baseball. Television. The televising of major-league games has given the alert, observant boy quick *visual* teaching of all the skills of the game, which has tremendously advanced and speeded Little League play and performance.

Faces in the Crowd

Look at these people—a neighborhood drawn together for one brief moment as they sit together behind third base. It is the bottom of the fifth in a close ball game. Study their faces: the seven-year-old boy with his hands prayerfully clasped in front of his chin, the two grandmothers in the front row, the young lovers holding hands at the upper left, the night watchman in front of them, the checker in the supermarket, the mothers, the Little League fathers, the one standing with the cap, the librarian, the telephone operator, the lady who works in the bakery, the baby sitter, the telephone-company man with the transistor radio, the insurance salesman behind him, the hysterical teen-age girl with her hands on her ears, and all the heads poking out from the last row. These are the faces at the instant of a mishap, their eyes, their nervous lips, their expressions of concern.

On the field a collision of two fielders on a pop fly! One lies motionless for a moment on the ground, and all the emotions of these people are reactions to the two boys. This is the face of the town. One heartbeat. A moment later the boys are on their feet and there is relief, laughter and applause for their effort (the catch was made and held). A few minutes later they are cheering. A double to deep left and the lead run. This same crowd drawn together for the drama of a game knows the whole gamut of expression.

These people are from Williamsport and they are watching a Little League World Series game. Their concern was not for their own neighborhood children but for two visiting youngsters from Hilo, Hawaii, 6,000 miles away. For boys they did not know or would never see again. Sometimes all boys and all neighborhoods are one.

Their Guy and Ours

For a fourteen-year-old standing on the hill in the bright sunshine of a Saturday morning in a game that decides the championship, there is a certain glory that somehow will never come again. *Then—* he is the best guy on the team, the pitcher, the star, and many times the best hitter too. The entire team knows this will be a showdown against the other team's best pitcher, and the game of baseball gains direction here: the inspirational force and leadership of the ace pitcher.

These boys are the starters in a Pony League final in Cincinnati. Organized in Pennsylvania in 1951 for graduates of Little League baseball to continue their development, the league plays all summer on a cut-down diamond, halfway in size (75 feet) between Little League and regulation. The official scorer *(left)* keeps a detailed record of every inning pitched in each game. The competition is keen, and it teaches boys during those two critical years, thirteen and fourteen, sportsmanship, teamwork, and self-reliance.

The well-coached, well-equipped, well-heeled boys at Yale enjoy the camaraderie of the dugout in an ivy-league game at New Haven.

Sun-tanned nomads in casual attire stand in shambles of Miami Beach High School practice session and gaze at palm trees in the outfield.

College Boys and Ragamuffins

These are boys from all families, rich or not, who enjoy an equality of opportunity on the diamond. The elite college boys and the tropical gashouse gang. The bubble-gum pinch hitter, son of a serviceman overseas; the center fielder in New Jersey who looks like Willie Mays and spends every hour believing he is; the handsome boy in a batting helmet playing American Legion ball in Ohio, or the Spanish first baseman with his enormous trap glove that cost as much as a suit of clothes.

To deter a student from leaving school on the bonus offer of a professional scout, baseball's new bonus rule prevents major-league teams from sign-ing college players until they have completed their sophomore year. In years to come, college players competing in summer *college leagues* may make a draft system for the majors a definite possibility.

At UCLA, Western Michigan, Yale, and other schools with top baseball programs, there is a dedication to fundamentals and play making. Fall practice prepares the boys for their twenty-five-game spring schedule. It is the best training a young baseball player could hope for because he receives the invaluable education he needs for life, whether he makes it in professional baseball or not. College should be the primary goal of a boy.

Run, Hit, Throw

It all comes down to these three things, from the four-year-old up through Little League to the leagues for older boys. The fire-department fellow is running out a triple in a Babe Ruth League game. The League was founded in 1952 for boys thirteen, fourteen, and fifteen years old who move up to the standard diamond of ninety feet between the bases. It is a big step upward. The sturdy moose at right is a Carolina pitcher in the new senior division of Little League for the same ages.

The original organized league for boys is American Legion baseball, begun in Milbank, South Dakota, in 1925. Frank McCormick, the state commander of the veterans group and athletic director of the University of Minnesota, proposed at that year's Legion convention a junior baseball program because boys were drifting away from the game. The program needed funds and appealed to Commissioner Landis and the league presidents for help. The majors agreed to underwrite the program up to $50,000 a year, and this subsidy has continued ever since. American Legion teams, for boys up to eighteen years old, playing in major-league parks (below), supply over half the total manpower to the majors!

Now the boys come of age physically and mentally, and their play takes on an added intensity. They begin to think seriously of baseball as a future. Playing for money.

Notes on a Tryout Camp

How DOES the big, strong, determined, but inexperienced kid pitcher on the preceding page get to a major-league team? He's seen by scouts and signed, if he's lucky! (I will discuss the entire scouting idea in Part III.) But what of the boys whose teams are not scouted? What chance have they for a future in baseball?

I believe very strongly in the local tryout camp idea for a major-league club. Here's my plan.

The announcement goes out on the date and site of the tryout for fifty boys. At nine A.M. on the first day every player fills out a complete information card. All boys then report to the clubhouse, where the club furnishes shirts only. Half are numbered from one to twenty-five in red—front and back—and the others have the same numerals in black. These shirts will be kept and used anywhere camps are held. Coaches wear full uniforms.

While the players are suiting up, each coach transfers the card information to clip sheets so that he is able to identify them when practice starts.

RUNNING: All the men run sixty-yard dashes, not to exceed four lanes, level ground, preferably on grass. Start the races from a side start, the same as off first base, with the left foot on a chalk line. The first two runners in each heat will be raced again, and if desirable, certain runners may be grouped for a third heat. The comparative running speed of every player will be known and his running form correctly appraised. A stop watch in the hands of an experienced timer helps.

THROWING: Then the men warm up. An arc is drawn in the outfield 260 feet from home plate. Each man is given six ground balls to be fielded and thrown back of the 260-foot mark, first three to a relay man placed at or near second base, then three to home plate. If the arm is good enough so that the relay man can either cut off the throw or let it go, in which latter case the ball reaches home plate on the first bounce, it is a *great* arm, and no one need look at it further.

Everybody throws: catchers, infielders, outfielders, first basemen—everyone except pitchers. Every coach marks his own clip sheet. The adjutant calls out with a megaphone the number of the man throwing, just as he calls out the numbers of the four runners in the races. Don't start a race and don't start a man throwing until all coaches are ready. At least twenty baseballs should be available in the outfield, so the boys throw continuously.

No man with a sore arm or with an ailing arm should be permitted to throw, and no man should be permitted to throw without being *well warmed up*. One of the coaches should be specifically designated to see to it that runners keep their legs warmed up and practice side-starting wherever they are standing in preparation for the races. Under no circumstances should the club be at fault for a pulled tendon, either in running or throwing, and this simply must not happen, *ever!*

Another observation about the throwing on the first day. The first round in throwing from the outfield, three throws, should be made to the relay man—then the second round can go to the plate, and the throwers should be called in rotation by their shirt number. This enables the boys to know when they will be called to the throwing line, and by then they can be completely warmed up.

There may be no infield or outfield practice during the first day. You cannot get to it. If the workout begins at ten A.M., the running and throwing should be and can be finished at twelve-thirty P.M. When these two exercises are finished, the pitching workouts begin. The other players go to lunch, and each pitcher goes to lunch as soon as he finishes his own workout. The pitcher candidates are worked individually on the sideline by an experienced person or preferably two such persons. Out of fifty men who are candidates for all positions, there will be from fifteen to twenty who will be pitchers. Some of the pitching candidates will be finished within a few minutes, but the time schedule should allow two hours for a fifteen-man pitcher workout that will come during the first day. Full dictation is made on all pitcher tryouts. A very good pitching prospect may take thirty minutes for his workout. This is an instructional period, but more particularly the workout is to test the aptitudes of the candidates and to get basic information on the pitchers' stuff.

AFTER LUNCH and after the pitching workouts are finished, the pitching machine and batting cage come into the picture. Each batsman hits three fair balls, and the men rotate in the batting cage according to their shirt number. Batsmen are judged on stride, hand and batting position, and other details that it is not necessary to discuss here, but with particular attention on the part of all coaches to the batsman's power. The clip sheet on batsmen will simply note two items—form and power. *Power: A,* average; *A+,* good; *A++,* very good; *A+++,* great; *A—,* not a prospect as a batsman. *Form: S,* satisfactory; *S+,* good; *S—,* faulty (and state reasons). This expresses a general idea of the markings.

The batting practice will probably take the rest of the afternoon, and the pitchers returning from lunch will be called for batting immediately upon their reporting, in accordance with their shirt numbers. All pitchers must be tried as batsmen. If hopeless batters appear (and in any free-agency group of fifty players not previously scouted, there are many), they should be excused from further appearance in the cage unless their running and throwing forbid this dismissal. A boy may be reporting, for example, as an infielder, and it is obvious that he cannot hit a lick and never will—but he might become a great pitcher. Bucky Walters of the Cincinnati Reds and many others have done just that. But the coaches, after or during the batting practice, can perhaps dismiss as many as half a dozen or possibly a dozen players, who will not be required to report the following day because they are not good enough.

WHEN the long day is finished, the coaches have a well-deserved meal and then a meeting at which every single player is fully discussed. The dismissals will reduce the group to half the size the second day. Club officials should attend these meetings and note top prospects. Complete coaching notes are written on each player on their respective clip sheets.

The next morning two teams are formed.

All infielders in the preliminary game practice rotate at third, shortstop, and second, so that every infielder is thoroughly seen as a shortstop. Likely-looking hitting pitchers can be played in the outfield or wherever needed. No practice anywhere (even in the running or the throwing on the first day, nor during the batting-cage work in the first day) is to be interrupted or delayed by any coach or anybody for the purpose of instruction. It is not an instructional camp in any sense and *should not* be. It is held and conducted for the purpose of observing players and evaluating their future. The infield practices are to begin the second day, and when fully completed, the outfield workout follows, with only three outfielders working at a time.

The game on the second day should not be confined to nine innings. If there are enough pitchers, the game might go eighteen innings. Each pitcher should be allowed to pitch at least one inning and should continue until the staff has seen enough of him to make a judgment about his future. Seldom does a pitcher work more than three innings. If there is a scarcity of pitchers, however, then the pitcher could go six or more if desirable. Every boy in the camp must know at the end of the two days that he has had a real tryout.

The management of these free-agency camps has been progressively organized, starting about forty years ago in the Cardinal organization under the direction of Charles Kelchner, Joe Schultz, Joe Mathes, Eddie Dyer, and Charles Barrett, and in later years, Rex Bowen, Wid Mathews, Andy High, George Sisler, Bob Clements, Howie Haak, Branch Rickey, Jr., and indeed several others. I have had an opportunity in these closely organized free-agent trials to prove to myself that you can clear one hundred men (not previously scouted) in a two-day camp, beginning at nine A.M. on the first day and ending at five P.M. on the second day. And you can have written opinions about every one of the hundred men. The two days' workout initially requires full paperwork: an adjutant on the field and not less than four men with designated supervisory duties during both days.

The idea of bringing these previously unscouted boys in for this two-day trial camp is absolutely wonderful. If this sort of thing could be done about three times a year, say from the first of June to the first of July, it could be the most valuable scouting opportunity I can think of. For many years I held these camps in many areas. In the earlier days, I have had as many as 300 report— *none previously scouted*. In the later years, with the intense scouting on the part of all major-league clubs, these camps have dwindled in numbers very much and most major-league clubs have abandoned them altogether.

With the enormously active Little League, Pony League, Babe Ruth, and American Legion baseball clubs in the United States these tryouts would be a popular challenge and opportunity for young prospects. The hope would be to sign one out of ten and have them report to the club's winter training base. Why not give every unscouted boy a chance to play baseball?

I remember so well at the close of the college year in 1903, when I was leaving my old home in the hills of southern Ohio to report to the Dallas Club in the Texas League as a player, that my mother, kneeling in prayer, asked God to give some special kindly protection for her son. It was really stronger than that. She almost gave advice to her Heavenly Father. She felt that I was going into a very worldly association. And in 1903 she was right.

I have a young seventeen-year-old grandson. He very recently pitched a no-hit game in his high-school league and only yesterday, as I write this, struck out eighteen batsmen in an American Legion seven-inning game in California. It so happens that he is a straight *A* student, especially strong in mathematics. He has entered as a freshman in an outstanding small college in California. If he shows sufficient ability, I shall do everything I can to have him go into professional baseball in America. There is no profession more worthy.

Spring Training

Like baseball itself, spring training was not invented. It evolved. Competition in the 1880's was such that one unnamed owner decided to steal a march on rivals by going far enough south for practice games in early April, then in late March, and soon the panic was on. Frank Bancroft pioneered with the Cincinnati club in Cuba. Florida, though primitive, became popular as early as 1890. I recall taking my St. Louis Browns there in 1914 and launching St. Petersburg as a baseball-training site. Our beginning was modest, but several features of our so-called mass training that year—batting cages, sliding pits, compulsory walking to and from the grounds—were retained and embellished through the years until we prepared as many as 743 contract players of all classifications, 300 in one camp. It all led up to today's "luxury" described in the following pages. Only the aches and perspiration, the shouts and crack of the bat are the same.

Grunts and Groans on the First Days

No last-place team, it seems to me, can rely on the play of fortune to bring to hand suddenly and without cause a coterie of great players. Neither is it safe for managers or coaches to feel they are so resourceful and superior either in selection or observation of players that by their own super-excellence they can bring a last-place club into contending position. Winning begins with fitness.

The early exercises in spring training give a few days of muscular soreness to some, who have not stayed in top shape through the winter, but the condition wears off within a few days. Calisthenics have been perfected under experienced direction so that complete routines with and without the bat bring every set of muscles into play. Baseball is a game of quick, sudden, lunging moves from a

standing rest position, and the young players' muscle tone must be conditioned and ready.

More men are put out of commission at spring training by side diversions or outside activities than from scheduled exercises afield. More casualties occur from sunburn and the common cold than anything else, unless it is the indulgences of the party man. I've seen the mixture of alcohol and professional baseball for sixty years. They don't mix. This is to the advantage of the player, and total abstinence is the only sensible safeguard. And finally, the most censurable and unforgivable deterrent to successful play is brash overweight. Physical fitness is a jealous factor in the life of every professional player, and any necessary price should be willingly paid to achieve it.

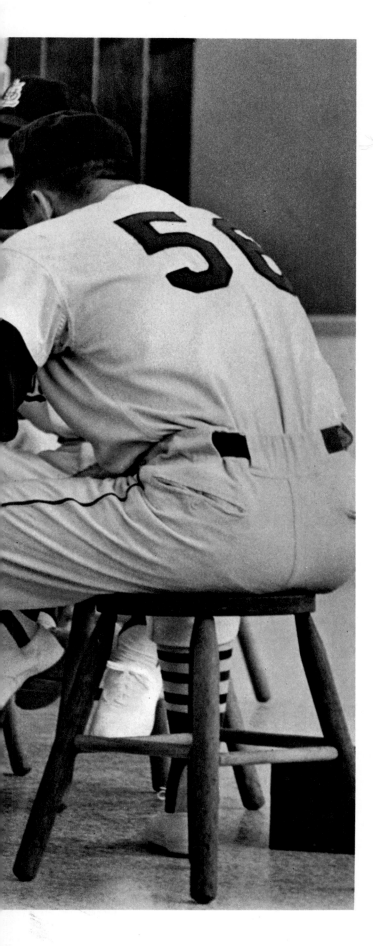

The Rookies

About sixty years ago I went to a major-league training camp. We had bats and balls and meager equipment. We reported on the field at ten A.M. and we worked until about twelve-thirty P.M. Everybody took a turn at bat, except pitchers. Each man would hit in turn four or five times, a maximum of say fifteen fair balls. Half of those fair hits in that day, as in this, would be hit on bad pitched balls—pitched outside the strike zone. The pitchers were soon worn out and the batting practice was over. Then we warmed up and took infield practice and outfielders shagged for fifteen minutes and we called it a day. Thirty days of that routine completed spring training.

In some major-league camps in those days, managers had two workouts, but most had only one. Managers had no coaches and gave little or no personal instruction or criticism to any player. The boy either had it or he didn't have it. He made the team or he didn't make it. He was pretty much a law unto himself and went his own way. If some day or other he saw another player of recognized ability doing something more effectively or more gracefully or more easily than he was doing it, he might elect to imitate him, and thus, by observation, in time he would improve himself.

In recent years, major-league managers have been provided with as many as half a dozen coaches —men of experience and pedagogical training and well-known ability and, too, of considerable prestige. In some modern camps in late years, such coaches were given teaching assignments, and each individual player was studied and his needs set out in writing for camp attention and program. If one of the rookies with the high numbers (at right) has the ability today, the club will find it out. He has a chance. Young players with weaknesses are given special tasks to be done over and over again. Most weaknesses of ballplayers are results of bad habits, and it takes time and continuous practice to break a bad habit and more time to acquire and gracefully use a new one.

These techniques, may I call them, are little items, but in the aggregate they spell the difference between major-league and minor-league players. This difference is by no means necessarily a difference in age, or in poundage, or in running speed, or in strength of arm, or in batting power, or in many other mentionable personal qualities. Many players in the minor leagues can run faster or hit harder than many boys in the majors. Aptitudes, attitudes, and effort, all capped by *desire,* may count as much as differences in physical abilities.

First Day in the Cage

The veteran possibly needs batting practice just as much as the rookie. The picture at left shows Red Schoendienst, an honored veteran of twenty years and new manager of the Cardinals, at bat in the batting cage. The rookie needs confidence, which he will doubtless acquire with orientation. The passing veteran has confidence and cannot understand why he doesn't hit with earlier skill. His instant reflexes, eyes particularly, are unconsciously impaired. He must labor in the batting cage to make adjustments. No longer can he pull the power stroke to his own field. This is the first mark of prowess failure in the great power hitters. He goes on the trading block even when the press and public are still idolizing him as the same great slugger. They hung me in effigy on the steps of Borough Hall the day I traded Dolph Camilli. Almost two years in advance of his leaving the majors, Camilli could no longer pull the ball over the right-field fence with former ease. The flight went to center, then left center, then left field. Well do I remember the day when Clark Griffith told Ty Cobb that he, Cobb, couldn't hit to right field any more. Griff was not entirely correct, but the long ball to dead right was no longer the common stroke for Tyrus Raymond. In that respect, Griff had him right. It's a painful day when a ballplayer realizes this truth.

So, indeed, the veteran in the fading era of his batting life needs the batting cage more than ever. He may practice stepping back with his rear foot instead of advancing with his front foot to hit to the opposite field. He loses power but remains just as dangerous.

The greatest single difference between a major-league and a minor-league player is the difference in his judgment of the strike zone. The major-leaguer knows better the difference between a ball and a strike and is better able to control his action as to whether to swing, hold up or "take" a pitch.

Suppose a fellow is graceful in handling a fork, but very improper in his use of a spoon. Well, one solution for such a person would be to give him only food that requires the fork. But it happens in baseball that pitchers also serve soup. To have a boy in camp for six weeks doing only the things he does well anyhow and never doing anything at all on the only thing that keeps him from being absolutely great is in my book a travesty and a very unintelligent approach to his problem.

Playmaking Drills

Iron Mike, the pitching machine, is the best drill-master in camp. It can throw the ball with varying speeds. It can produce different rotations or none at all. In other words, it can simulate several pitches of the human arm. The batsman is not in danger of injury. The machine can pitch to the batsman's weaknesses with considerable regularity. The batsman can umpire the pitches. He can present himself to the pitch and hold up, then debate with a coach or another batsman as to whether the pitch was in the strike zone. Bunting form can be taught against a pitching machine *(previous page)* better than it can against a human machine because the pitches are buntable and the coaching opportunity is much better. Instructions can be given more privately or a player work out alone.

In spring training camps the batter, after long practice from the pitching machine, may finally come to know that a certain pitched ball, continuously thrown with varying speeds into the zone that is doubtful as to height and width, is a bad pitch, although it may be a pitch that he has been assuming for years was good. His confidence mounts because he is now able to get the count to two and nothing or three and one, where for years he has been continually in the hole. Acquiring a workable knowledge of the strike zone is very helpful to a man with a bat in his hands, particularly if his salary in thousands of dollars depends upon it. But it is even more valuable—even revolutionary—for the manager and coach. Study and instruction can be carried out miraculously well in a small fraction of the time that used to be spent.

In modern spring training camps, almost without exception, a full routine of intelligent practice drills in one direction or another has been adopted. In the pictures below an electrically operated air gun fires line drives to the outfield, to pinpoint positions in the alley or down the line, or makes bloop singles, or sends deep flys to an exact spot in center field. The coach using it simulates any hit, and then the "batter" leaves the plate as a runner and the outfielder practices his throws to second or the plate. The first baseman works on the cutoff or the second baseman on the relay. The results duplicate game conditions exactly.

Or take the practice where five or six pitchers rotate in pitching to a phony batsman. The batsman lets the ball go by, and when the catcher catches it—or, indeed, perhaps a fifth of a second before—a smart coach (the phony batsman) taps another ball with his fungo bat. This smart coach-batsman can bunt the ball along the third-base line or to the right toward first base, or he can drive the ball with varying speeds back through the pitcher's box, or he can hit it to the first baseman. The pitcher doesn't know what this smart coach will do, and he is therefore required to follow his pitch and come to a fielding position instantly upon delivering the ball. The pitcher is supposed to field the ball whether it is hit along the third-base line, the first-base line, or back to him. The slow-driven ball toward first offers a choice to the pitcher whether to cover first or make the play. He must make the decisions, and, of course, he must cover first on balls fielded by the first baseman. In the course of thirty minutes, this practice provides an opportunity for at least five pitchers, and as many first basemen, to correct their bad habits and develop their instinctive techniques.

In this day, surely, it is an indictment of camp management if players who might have been helped in a given year have not been brought through until two or three years later. It is also a career tragedy in the life of the player, who might have helped himself.

There are two ways a young player develops. The first is by the player's own observation. He copies or learns from other players. This ordinarily is a slow, self-elected process, and it requires an average of three to five years of such apprenticeship in the minor leagues in order to reach a regular major-league job. The other method is that of personal attention and instruction, usually by conversation or lecture or field demonstration. It is by this procedure that a player acquires the skills of a position. He loses bad form at bat and may become an artistic and effective batsman. The player is directed toward improvement, and then by his own application becomes efficient at the earliest possible time. It is a much faster educational process by which men are required to devote themselves to their weaknesses.

Baseball is a science—indeed, it is an art—and there is a scientific approach that makes the observation method antiquated. A man in this profession should be compelled to learn to do well the things that are helpful in bringing him toward some standard of perfection. He must bring his abilities up to his capabilities.

The Clubhouse

There was a day when there wasn't a clubhouse like this. Fresh air—ventilation—air conditioning—infrared lights—waxed vinyl floors—medical gadgets and equipment such as electrically controlled vibration machines and whirlpool baths. I doubt if any profession or industry provides more expert medical specialists, not only in the field of injury but in all human illnesses, than professional baseball. Doctors who favor Father Time as a curative for ills or injuries are the greatest enemy of a pennant winner. It is more or less common belief in the medical profession that rest is the very first prescription. I don't dispute it, but I happen to know that the game scheduled for tomorrow cannot be postponed until Christmas if the hangnail on poor Bill's finger keeps him from taking his turn as scheduled. That game can go in the loss column ahead of time, two days or more before it is played. A medical-school graduate with an osteopathic degree—if that were possible—who desired to win the pennant as much as the manager would possibly be the most valuable employee a major-league owner could have on the payroll.

The club trainer is a much underrated adjunct to most teams. He's the clearing house of all troubles, financial and domestic, and perhaps also of all secrets and unnecessary illnesses. A good one has the confidence of all the players—he earns it and holds it. He should have a close fiduciary relationship with the players. Bucks Weaver, the Cardinal trainer for twenty-five years, was a great practical philosopher, a student and teacher of all the facets that make for team morale.

Team morale is the salvation of team slumps and is a worthy objective of team management and particularly of front-office planning. The team that has the most of it in late August is usually the strongest pennant threat. An additional incentive is team pride. Public acclaim, newspaper comment, prospective distinction in a World Series, all are helpful. Any one of these many times offer an even more lasting cohesive than money.

The picture above shows the spot where team morale goes to bat. If you visit a clubhouse in the spring, look over the faces and cock your ear for snatches of conversation, and you will get an advance revelation of where the team is headed. The clubhouse is the sanctuary of morale.

I like this picture. You would think the white boy is consoling or advising the colored boy. Nothing of the sort! This picture has a surprising significance—the colored boy is consoling the white boy.

That's a new day in this game of baseball.

These boys' lockers join. The white boy is down and doesn't care what happens, and the colored boy is taking him to task. I know both boys very well. The colored boy is William White, twenty-seven years of age, a great first baseman and an extra-base .300 hitter on the St. Louis Cardinals. He holds a B.A. degree from a highly creditable college, Hiram in Ohio. He has experience in the game and his spiritual companion is good will. The white boy is a rookie pitcher with arm trouble, and a bad day. He is discouraged. There is no patronizing—White is trying to help—offering a word of encouragement.

In baseball, racial discrimination is over the hill. "Physical proximity," says Professor Tannenbaum of Columbia, "works its way against all seemingly absolute systems of values and prejudices."

Proximity will help solve it, but we cannot have enough of it. It takes time, a long time, too much time. It's a long road from legal right to moral acceptance, but in baseball, full racial equality is a fact. The black man in sport is not a Negro American citizen. He is simply an American citizen.

"Let's Take Him Along"

A major-league camp has sixty players. The player limit is forty. The club would like to go North reduced to thirty. At the left is the saddest picture in the book. These are two boys who have just received notice of reassignment to a minor-league club. I know the facts about one of them. He hasn't given up and he just doesn't know how to remake his plans. He has been baseball-minded since childhood. He says he knows nothing else — like Honus Wagner or Satchel Paige. He can run and he can throw and he has power with a bat in his hands. He has aptitude. Orientation ought to follow very fast. Maybe it will. Look out for him.

It can be a great mistake to send this boy to the minor leagues. The club may want him back before the end of the year—at mid-season or earlier—and that might be difficult or even impossible because of the player limit or because the option

list is full. The club has a deadline date of thirty days after the opening of the season to cut down to its player limit of twenty-five. If there is ever a time in the life of a manager when he needs to pray for wisdom, it comes when he faces the cut-down. Perhaps it would be better to take him along. There is no "give up" with this fellow. He is the first man in the clubhouse and the last man off the field. He has the fourth qualification of a major leaguer—he loves to play.

Take my case: I promised to marry Jane in June if I made good. Everything depended upon it. I did make good and was married on the first day of June. But the depths of despair that come to boys such as this one, who has spent three full years in the minor leagues, are for some hours indescribable. Usually he goes away with a renewed determination, and a realistic faith substituted for hope.

93

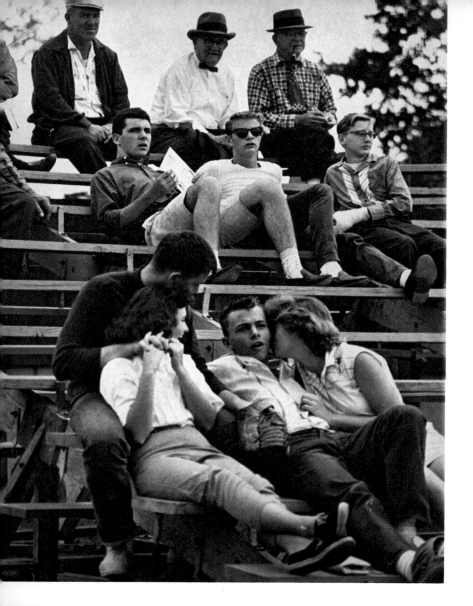

Grapefruit Game

When the teams are shaping up they visit each other in March at their nearby training sites to play an exhibition schedule of games. It is the first test for the pitchers to go five, seven, then nine innings. The first test for the hitter and the fielder to go all out. The chance for the crowds to see intraleague games, old stars, and bonus kids. The fans are mostly the retired old folks who love baseball, especially the ladies, who look forward to watching the games on the grapefruit circuit each year, and the young boys, who bring their gloves and get as close to their heroes as they can, for there is no major-league ball in their city, only TV. In the center-field bleachers *(left)* you may find three generations of fans. Grandpa, Dad, the college boy, and the teen-age lover. The girl at right whispers sweet nothings into the ear of the boy. The girl at left affectionately holds the throwing hand of her boy friend while he wears a glove on his left hand waiting for a fly ball. The atmosphere is relaxed and friendly. Behind the rookie outfielder's worried look, three pitchers get in shape by running wind sprints *(lower left)*. The first game of the season is just a week away. When the teams move north, the games begin to count.

In deepest center behind the grass cutter local boys have their own game hitting mashed-up paper cups with a board.

Boys edge out from behind fence to be on field as one reaches into his pal's popcorn box without missing a pitch.

Courage

I THINK that we must understand one another when we talk about guts, which is the field term for courage. My first reflection is that courage is relative. We're inclined to call youngsters yellow when as a matter of fact they don't lack intestinal fortitude at all, they lack orientation. They lack acquaintanceship; they have an initial timidity that comes from a lack of a sense of at-homeness. Sometimes it is a great quality in men to show modesty even to the point of timidity or apparent lack of courage.

We judge them too quickly. A great many boys when they are not on the field can be very strong and very firm and very aggressive, as a matter of fact. Enos Slaughter was afraid to say his name. George Sisler was and is by nature a listener, but he has never compromised his beliefs by word or action. This is the essence of courage. Paul Dean had no capacity to build the Panama Canal, but he had an adequate supply of blind pitcher's mound guts—as much as Dizzy. There was no place in his brain for the comprehension of fear.

The signs of courage are not players that yell. I believe in players who are by nature a bit vociferous and speak their piece. I believe in players who don't say a word. I believe in players being *positively themselves*—not trying to call on a resource they don't have, nor putting on something extraordinary when they don't feel it. You want people to be real. You want them to be just the way they feel.

Don't ever put it down that the quiet fellow is not smart or resourceful. They have great courage, and sometimes a man who never says a word is the man who never overlooks a single possible advantage he might take in the game. They are great players; they are wonderful players. Vocalization is not the test of courage. It has very little, indeed, to do with it.

There is a moral courage and there is a physical courage. Many men will not dare to risk opinion where it is likely to be considered unpopular or to risk a judgment on any issue where there is likely to be a prevailing sentiment on the other side. They will keep quiet about a wrong procedure and perhaps endure it to their own disadvantage. It's a lack of moral courage. The same person, however, if you were to offend him in some of his physical prerogatives, if you were to be personal with him—if you called him a name or assaulted him in some way—he would fight back instantly, lacking no physical courage. Fight to the last ditch? Possibly so. Some people believe that players who do not have the ultimate in physical courage do not have the ultimate in moral courage. That is not true. Jess Haines would not throw at a batsman regardless of provocation. Jackie Robinson had the moral courage to turn the other cheek. Many professional players do that. But a man who is not willing to support alone a principle that he believes in usually has no physical courage. True!

Secondly, there is a relationship in my judgment between experience and courage. Dumbness, obtuseness, lack of knowing what to do and how to do it—unalertness—can sometimes be interpreted so easily as yellowness. It's easy for us to say that. But in all my years in baseball I've heard of only one coward. All the others that the boys say are yellow—I say that it's a lack of acquaintanceship with people or surroundings, a lack of experience. As soon as they get acquainted and know their way around, there aren't very many boys who come up to us in baseball who are really yellow.

VERY, *very* few boys really are what you could call physically and morally afraid—cowards. I don't think they reach the major leagues. They don't ordinarily make the high-school baseball or football team! They don't get that far. I don't think so. And it's not a characteristic of human nature—really—to be afraid. You're always sensitive to circumstances around you that are full of threats or danger either to your opinions or to your actions. I know that is true. But when men get over that they come to themselves.

A winning desire, the unquenchable urge that some ballplayers have for victory—utilizing nerve and courage—this, of course, is never questioned.

The man who evidenced the greatest degree of physical courage that I ever knew in the game of baseball was Cobb himself. He didn't really have more courage, if there were ways to measure it, in the field of moral standards or physical standards; he probably had no more than a great many men I could name. But he had that carelessness about showmanship; such utter disregard of the sportive rights of competitors that he violated them and let the chips fall where they would, and he had deservedly the reputation of being a very aggressive player. Courage, yes. Guts, they call it. Yes. Of course he was unafraid. But he had superlative skills and ability with it and they enabled him to do things that others didn't and couldn't do. Skill puts the chrome on courage. Then if you add desire you have a Traynor or a Lillis or indeed most teams' winning players. It is undeniable that desire and courage go together.

THERE IS a story that I can tell you on this point. It concerns a game that we played against the Boston club some years ago. Jim Bottomley was the first baseman, and Rogers Hornsby was the second baseman and followed Jim in the batting order. It was in the heyday of Cardinal greatness. In late season this fellow Bottomley had a bad slider on his hip—it was a terrible thing—and he had been having it treated for some time. It was infected and the doctor had Jim stripped on his table. Before the game, Captain Shotten came to me and said, "I don't think Jim can play." I said, "Why not?" "Well," he says, "have you seen his leg?" I said, "No, I didn't see it, but I know about it." And he said, "Well, come in here and look at it." We took a look, the doctor had Jim stripped on the table—it was a nasty sight. He was lying on his side and I said, "Jim, can you play?" He said, "Why sure, I think I can play." And so I turned to Shotten when we went out of the room and I said, "Just leave his name in the lineup and if he appears on the field to practice let him play." Jim took one round of practice and Shotten handed his name in. I said to him as the game was about to begin, "If you have to slide, protect that right side. Don't slide on it."

In the ninth inning, Jim got on first by a base on balls and there were two men out and the score was a tie. Hornsby was at bat. Jim knew it was tactically necessary—he had to steal—and on his own he set sail for second.

The throw was low and a bit on the third-base side of the second-base bag, and of course the baseman's position is determined by the throw. I saw Jim take off on a vicious abandoned slide to the right—on the damaged hip. Maranville, the Boston shortstop, made the tag, a very close play. The umpire called Jim safe.

The crowd was cheering. You could have heard a pin drop on our bench. Jim got up slowly. I saw him pull his trousers away from his hip three or four times as he took his lead with half a limp. He tugged at his trousers again.

I had made a talk at the morning meeting about paying the price for the thing you wanted. You didn't get something for nothing. You had to pay. You never get anything out if you don't put something in.

Instantly on the decision, a young pitcher, John Stuart of Ohio State football and baseball fame, standing on the front of the dugout, put drama into the situation. John cupped his hands and with a clarion voice called out twice: "He paid the price! He paid the price!"

Johnny Stuart put glassy eyes on every man of us. Hornsby scored Bottomley with a line drive over second and won the game.

In the clubhouse with Jim on the trainer's table, I asked, "How in the name of common sense did you come to slide on that bad hip? I told you to slide on the other side." He just looked up with the strangest and most surprised stare in the world as though he were amazed at the question. He said, "Mr. Rickey, didn't you see where Maranville was standing?" My soul, if he had gone to the right directly into Maranville's hands and directly into the throw—Maranville was taking the throw over on the left side—he would have been out! "Don't you see where Maranville was then? What was the difference about my leg? What was the difference about anything? I've got to go to the left, away from the play, away from the tag. It makes no difference what happens to me. Maybe this is the ball game!"

It's a marvelous thing—the telling question—"Didn't you see where he was standing?" The whole reason for action anywhere is what is the purpose of the play—what is the purpose of the game—what is it we're trying to do? What's the cost—what difference does it make what the cost is? Men who want something very much and find what it is they want, if they're dealing in any kind of an honest world, they'll not question the cost or the price, and they probably won't ask it. I want it! I need it! It's just what I'm looking for! What's the cost? There is no cost. Whenever I get a team in this organization that doesn't ask the price, that says "I want victories; I want distinction; I want the World Series; I want to win, legally, legitimately, sportingly," a team that asks no quarter from anybody and gives none either, then I know they have courage. Where's Maranville standing? We won that ball game. The end of the story is that Mr. Bottomley kept playing on the leg and never missed a single inning during that injury.

DESIRE makes men do everything. It makes men slide on an injured hip without question—it makes men come in at night without rules—it makes men honest with themselves and their families, and they hold certain fidelities very dearly. It makes men do voluntarily what they can't do well. They approach a subject or a physical act that they have never done and know little about and can't do, and yet know they need to be specially proficient in.

If they want to be great, if they want to win, if they want to be identified with a great organization, they voluntarily tackle the thing they're weak in. That's one of the hardest jobs for a player. Trying to learn what is difficult for you or what you don't do well requires great moral courage.

Doing the thing that ought to be done, getting rid of indecision, *that* leads to championship.

Opening Day

The first day of the pennant race is something special. To the team it counts in the standings just as much as the final game in September, although it is difficult to remember the games you won or lost in early April when you're locked in a duel for the flag with only ten games to go. To the fans it is a day of spirited hope, a new beginning when the first buds of April herald the promise of spring and summer. The exhibition games have been reported in the local papers for some weeks and now the business men and women and the regular season fans all come out to get a look at the new shortstop or phenomenal rookie pitcher or their beloved veterans. On opening day it *is* next year! The year the home team can win. Hope springs eternal in April, when the President of the United States throws out the first ball.

It should be deeply gratifying to every American citizen that our nation's chief executive can take such a personal interest in the opening game. President William Howard Taft started the custom in 1910 at the opener in our Capitol. He too sensed this need for a symbol of a new beginning each year and for competitive sport in our society. Here then, half a century later on the opening day of the 1962 season, President John F. Kennedy with his characteristic life and spirit inaugurated the opening of the magnificent new D. C. Stadium as Washington played Detroit (below). John Kennedy sat in the presidential box to the left of the home-team dugout and with a capacity crowd watched

another baseball season begin. The President has a score card in his hands, opened on the score sheet of the home club, and he has an uncapped pen ready for use. He has been able to keep a proper score since he was fifteen years of age. Within a few minutes, he will throw out the first ball.

No player knows as he steps to the plate for the first time in the opening game what kind of a year he will have. He may be injured and have a poor year, he may be traded to another club, he may have a good year, or he may have before him a remarkable season for a professional in sport.

The season soon swings into high gear, and the young boys we saw on the Little League diamonds come out to the ball park to see the professionals. Their team! Their center fielder! The picture on the next pages invades their promised land in the upper deck in left field.

What do you think was going on on the field? Was a player down with possible injury? Was an error part of it? Was there an umpire ruckus? Here's integration without riots, legislation or controversy. Here's neighborhood gradations of people, vertical slices of a community having fun and no one inquiring about flat shins or cephalic measurements. The scorecard salesman, the knot-holers, from across the tracks and the interested young ladies—no one's out of place. The old man in the left-hand corner is a juryman not ready to vote. *Here's the meaning of baseball as the national game in a "land of the free."*

Nine Men Alone

It all begins with that one man alone—the pitcher. Standing with his foot on the rubber, his shoulders hunched and the ball hidden behind his thigh, he looks in for the signal. He is set to pitch. The dusty gold circle of the mound is his world, and to 50,000 spectators in the park he is the dominant figure. The stark expanse of the hill cruelly accentuates his responsibility when he is in trouble, but it is a brilliant stage when he is masterfully in control.

The catcher raises his glove to check the position of the sun, so that he may maneuver under a pop fly behind the plate and not be blinded. The first batter steps into the batter's box. The batsman carefully places his rear foot in the dirt that certain distance from the back line that is best for him and the exact distance from the far side of home plate that will enable his bat, extended in a full swing, to cover the strike zone. The batsman sets himself, looks out to the pitcher, and is ready. He is on his own and alone in the box. This is the great, simple drama of the game of baseball. The moment when pitcher and batter face each other.

Inches

In center field the speck of white, alone in a vast openness of green playing field, waits and watches until the instant the ball is hit. Then, with incredible swiftness, he races to that precise point in the outfield to meet the trajectory of the ball and make the catch.

The infielder moves to his left or right as the batted ball explodes at him, the first baseman lunges to the foul line and misses the line drive in a puff of white chalk.

It seems preposterous, when you see the nine men separated, that the distance between the three outfielders and the six men on the diamond will be erased as they match their skills against the measured geometry of the field. The game comes down to inches as the left fielder races into the corner to catch a towering fly just inside the foul pole.

Against the enormous scope of a stadium and its tens of thousands of voices there is the artful detail of the game of baseball. The strong still hands on the end of the bat, expressing the total power of a hitter, the ball at the precise moment it spins off the tops of a pitcher's blurred fingers and begins its accurate arc to that spot above the plate. Now play begins.

105

The Hitters

When a scout is looking for a good batsman, he must have two qualities in mind—hitting form and power. If a batsman has good form and good power he should become a good hitter. If, possessing both, he still has trouble getting the bat and ball together, he should have his eyes examined. No one can make the major leagues without normal vision. Eyeglasses have become an invaluable aid to modern hitters. Tommy Davis, who led the National League in batting for two years, wears glasses, as do Bill Virdon, Frank Howard, catcher John Roseboro, and many others. Years ago this was unheard of. Some scouts include courage as a prerequisite for prospective hitters. Of course players must not be afraid to stand up to the plate, but this thing called courage is possessed by most prospective batsmen if they have good form. Courage is the by-product of form. Form is the horse and courage is the cart.

The Simmonses and Groats and Musials and the many others whose initial position in the batter's box seems to indicate to the uninitiated that the batting form is unusual or even bad in no sense disprove the statement that form in batting is most important. Preliminary stance at the plate means nothing at all. A moving picture of the batter's position at the time the ball leaves the pitcher's hand can determine his form. Where his front foot may be in the preliminary position is not worthy of attention. The hand movement, the level sweep of the bat, the length of the stride, the head movement—this is what's important when the pitch is on.

First and most important is the stride. I have never known a definite overstrider to make good as a regular in the major leagues. If the batsman does the split, he should either go to pitching or go back home. What constitutes an overstride is debatable, but the definite overstrider cannot be corrected. I have had this matter under discussion many times with baseball managers, including Mr. McGraw and Mr. Mack, without disagreement.

All the great batsmen were what would be termed short striders. One of the very great hitters of all time, Joe DiMaggio, frequently in raising the front foot would set it back down almost exactly in the same spot in the batter's box.

The second thing that gets my attention in the field of good form is the big end of the bat—where it is and what it does at the time the ball leaves the pitcher's hand. If it wiggles very much, that's bad. The big end of the bat must be still and as far back as it can go before making the forward swing.

There must be no hitch in the initial move of the bat. If a batsman has a hitch (the dropping of the hands while the ball is in flight), the big end of the bat will likely go in two directions—first back and then forward. It is difficult enough to hit great pitching by moving the bat in one direction. Going in two directions it's impossible. Practically every great batsman in the history of the game had no dip or motion with the big end of the bat preliminary to the forward sweep. A small coin would not prematurely fall off the big end of the bat with most of the great hitters.

Another feature of batting is the direction of the sweep of the bat. The level sweep is good. Any variation is correspondingly bad, and unless the batter has extraordinary power to hit the ball over the fence with his normal swing, the fly-ball hitter is out of luck. The level sweep of the bat will of course give any batsman a normal number of fly balls, say half and half with ground balls. A Ruth could be an uppercutter, as all typical home-run hitters *could* be, without directing too much adverse criticism to his form. However, the so-called home-run hitters are, in general, not uppercutters.

Some hitters strike out more than they should. I remember a training camp in Bradenton, Florida, when a young and inexperienced Class D manager present in the camp told a big freshman recruit who had struck out eight of the last ten times in squad games, "John, do you know what's the matter with you?" John, a big 200-pounder who could hit the ball over any fence when he hit it at all, just looked at the young manager. "I can tell you what the matter is with you, John—you strike out too much. You have got to cut that out." Conclusions on acknowledged faults can hardly change the efforts of any neophyte. No one wants to strike out!

A great fault of many young managers is over-coaching, overmanaging, over-pointing out an instinctive fault without implementing a cure. It doesn't do any good to tell a young player that he doesn't run fast enough. That won't enable him to run faster. The striking-out cure is effected, if at all, without ever mentioning striking out to the batsman. Put him in the cage and give the pitching machine high velocity and tell the batsman to hit *good* balls *with intent*. That's the cure.

The three panels at the left describe clearly hitting with intent. Notice all the strength it takes for Mickey Mantle to check his swing, not to break his wrists at the last instant when a good pitch is just out of the strike zone. With full power Jim Gentile (*center*) connects solidly as his wrists roll over in the completed swing. Elston Howard (*below*) nicely places bat to ball in a perfect bunt by a power hitter. All these men are in control. They are on the offense with that bat.

There is a fairly unanimous agreement that the best cure for abnormal striking out is to make the batsman practice pushing or pulling the ball with every swing. McGraw always insisted that if a batsman tried to hit the ball to his opposite field or to pull it to his own field, he would get a piece of it. Such a batsman may sacrifice some power in his stroke, but he seldom misses the ball. For many years I have experimented with batsmen in the effort to improve contact with the ball with every swing. McGraw was one hundred percent right!

A batsman's extremity can be and usually is the coach's first opportunity to help him. Premature correctives before a batsman gives up or seeks advice can bring everlasting excuse for failure, and the adviser carries the burden of cause for ever. Don't try to change batsmen until they are ready to be helped. Young managers are usually too quick to correct faults.

Batsmen are not simply born good or bad. Except for the overstrider, batsmen can be improved very much and in several directions. Power hitting *is* considerably dependent upon inheritance. You either have power or you don't have it. It is not acquirable.

I have watched baseball for sixty years. I've never heard of any ballplayer adding power. I've never seen a young boy come up to the major leagues who could not hit with power and watched the coaches work with him and then seen the day come when he would hit with power. You cannot *add* power. You cannot add it to a batter or a runner or a pitcher or put it in the arm of an outfielder. A man is born with power. And that is it. You can correct a hitch in a batter's swing and so increase his hitting ability and bring to bear power that was being wasted, but you cannot add power. You can teach a man who has power to use it—and that is an art. Power is inborn, and its control and explosive use are instinctive. When you see power on the diamond it is as clear as a cannon shot.

Such is the general opinion of baseball managers concerning a hitter's power. But most players do improve in batting as time goes on, and almost all players can be helped with good instruction and plenty of practice.

Batting was a perfect science for Tyrus Raymond Cobb. So it was for Sisler. Read his book on the subject. It was for Speaker and Collins. Both were student batsmen. I call your attention to the preparatory care and precision of approach, foot position, hand extension, and the exact bat location at the final moment when the batsman presents himself to the pitch. The instant coordination of almost all the muscles of the entire body to do one single simple little thing: Hit an elusive round ball with a round bat. That's batting.

Ted Williams

It is safe to say that considering their total abilities as hitters in the last two decades the four batsmen on these pages rank with any four hitters in baseball history. Each man is different, but each has dedication and power, intent, and intelligence in an unparalleled degree. Williams, Mantle, Mays and Musial. They are the big hitters in baseball whom people pay to see. They are worth the price of admission, and once you watch them you never forget them, as you will never forget these marvelous pictures. Ted Williams' eyes and his gigantic figure, Mickey Mantle's personification of power,

Willie Mays' laughter and spirit and quickness, Stan Musial's stature and timeless grace.

Ted Williams would sit on the second step of the Red Sox dugout with his cap off and sun himself and study the hitters in the cage. He would learn something about hitting every day and help the young hitters on the other team right behind the cage if they asked his advice. When he stepped in the batting cage he cared for only one thing: to hit! How can a man with eyes like that not be a great hitter? His exceptional vision triggered his gargantuan swing *(next page)*.

.406

More than 8,000 men have played in the major leagues since 1900, but only eight of them have achieved a batting average of .400 during a season. One man in a thousand. Nap Lajoie, Ty Cobb, Joe Jackson, Rogers Hornsby, George Sisler, Harry Heilmann, Bill Terry, and the last man to achieve baseball's highest prize, Ted Williams, who hit .406 in 1941, shown here at the moment of his classic swing hitting one of his 521 home runs in Fenway Park. Cobb did it three times, and Hornsby hit over .400 two successive years in 1924 and 1925! When Jackson hit .408 in 1911 it wasn't even good enough to win the batting crown. Ted Williams came closest again in 1957 with .388 to prove his greatness near the end of his career.

Only eight hitters in the major leagues have hit .350 during the last 15 years. The majestic batting average of .400 is becoming a dream. Managers will tell you it's night baseball, plane travel, exceptional pitching, smart defenses, huge fielding gloves that steal away base hits, manicured ball parks and the financial reward of the home run. I believe there are ten men in the majors today who could hit .400 if they would try to hit the ball past the fielders and not out of the park.

In all the world of sport you see a man from time to time with that individual style and shape and gesture that makes him unique. It is true in baseball. It is true that each hitter is completely different although he does exactly what the next fellow does—just swing at the ball. They called Ted Williams the splendid splinter, and in this memorable photograph (left) of him leaving the plate, watching the flight of the ball, he looks it. He seems ten feet tall. You had to smile when you saw him hit. His enthusiasm for batting was conveyed with every gesture to the farthest corners of the ball park and to those watching on television. It was a severe disappointment when the pitcher walked him. He was too dangerous to pitch to. He led the American League in walks for eight seasons. Only Babe Ruth was purposely put on base more often, leading in eleven seasons.

The results of putting bat to ball are recorded in the box score of each game, and a batter's appearances at the plate divided by his base hits determines his average. In the unending duel between batter and pitcher the bat and the ball are always discussed and analyzed as a cause for power dominance or pitching mastery. The fact that a round ball traveling at ninety miles per hour with a spin that causes it to curve in flight is being hit with a round piece of wood that is only two and three-quarters inches wide at the thick end does not seem to be sufficient cause for fluctuating statistics to many people.

Babe Ruth not only changed modern baseball with his home-run hitting but he influenced bat design. Ruth, Cobb, Sisler and Speaker all used bats forty ounces or more in weight, but Ruth's home-run records began a trend to lighter bats. Other players wishing to emulate his swing and not having his girth or power decided they could duplicate his swing with lighter bats. Rogers Hornsby initiated modern bat styling and effected the transition from the old large-handled bats, with small barrel and the weight more evenly distributed, to the first modern bat. Hornsby's bat had a comparatively large barrel tapering gracefully to a small handle. When Babe Ruth took this shape and added his weight out at the head end of the bat and accentuated the gradually tapering handle, it added considerable whip when swung. Today the whip effect is more prominent than it ever was, because the handles are thinner than ever. Roger Maris' bat has a narrower handle than a Little Leaguer's bat.

Most bats are thirty-four to thirty-five inches long, but for the same length will be different weights according to the hitter's order. Ralph Kiner's bat was thirty-five inches long and weighed forty-two ounces. Another thirty-five-inch bat may weigh thirty-two ounces. The heavier bat will be better able to withstand the shock of each hit and will have more driving power, but the smaller player may get more bat speed with a lighter bat and so increase his driving force.

Mickey Mantle

There is no question that Mickey Mantle is the strongest hitter of all if only because he performs on one leg. He is a cripple. If he were sound he would have batted .400 by now and hit the ball out of Yankee Stadium. Consider one of the toughest competitors and finest pitchers in the American League in the last twenty years— Early Wynn. Nothing ever impressed him much. He always expected everybody to put out. Wynn had high regard for Mantle as a hitter, but it wasn't until he saw Mickey suiting up in the All-Star game dressing room one year that he really understood the Yankee outfielder's courage. "I watched him dress. I watched him bandage that knee—that whole leg—and I saw what he had to go through every day in order to play. And now I'll never be able to say enough in praise. Seeing those legs, his power becomes unbelievable." Casey Stengel, who despite his gruff professional attitude always admired Mantle, gave him even higher tribute. "Mantle is the only man I ever saw who was crippled who could outdo the world. If he plays four or five more years his record will be so good no one will ever believe he was a cripple!"

For the power he has, Mantle is the fastest man to first base and a most powerful slider. But his appeal to the baseball fan is his consistent power from either side of the plate, hitting either left-handed or right-handed with a magnificent swing (next page), and his ability to hit all pitchers and all pitches despite the grueling pain, which the fans have now taken for granted, but which the camera sees in the photograph taken during the fourth game of the 1961 World Series in Cincinnati. His injured hip was bleeding during the game and the Yankees played the final game without him. There have been countless players over the years who have had guts enough to outlast physical hurts, but few had the strength to help carry a championship team year after year while doing it.

Willie Mays

The fans watch their favorite hitters come to the plate, enjoying their every mannerism and facial expression, their every move in the batter's box. You know it's Mays for there will be a tremendous roar in Candlestick Park or anywhere around the league and Willie will smile in the sunshine and adjust his cap. He'll miss one and spin full around, he'll foul one off, he'll take a couple, and when the second pitch is close he'll freeze for a moment and wait for the call. He'll dig in and the pitcher will breeze one close and Willie will duck, and you won't forget the look in his eye. Then he'll laugh at the catcher's remark and you will think he is eighteen, although he was thirty when this picture above was taken. Then he'll step in and set himself for the three-and-two pitch and suddenly this loose, ebullient boy is a serious, intent hitter and the ball is there and Mays swings. Hit!

Willie Mays' true greatness is his equal strength hitting, running, and throwing and the intensity with which he executes every play. He is the only player to steal thirty bases and hit thirty home runs in a season. His single catch and throw in 1954 changed that World Series, and his throw to Westrum on August 15, 1951, to get Billy Cox at the plate began a miracle ending to his rookie year. He slid into Bruce Edwards in Ebbets Field one day and Edwards said Mays was the strongest man ever to hit him. If there was a machine to measure each swing of a bat it would be proven that Mays swings with more power and bat speed pitch for pitch, than any other player.

The memory of Willie as a rookie propelling the ball in one electric flash off the Polo Grounds scoreboard on the face of the upper deck in left field for a home run is a cherished image. The ball got up there so fast it was incredible. Like a pistol shot it would crash off the tin and fall to the grass

124

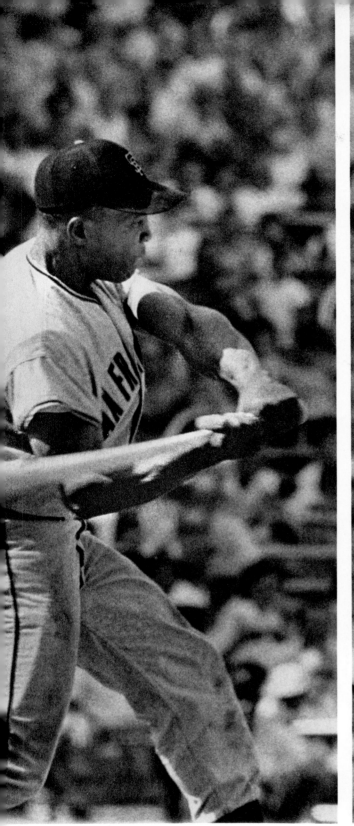

below. He would still have the knob of the bat in his huge hand and be but leaning in the direction of first base.

The sequence of three pictures above is the Mays swing. The ideal stride, the right elbow in close, the bat level, meeting the ball out in front of the plate. You can see clearly the leverage a hitter puts behind his swing, the supple strength of a batter's wrists. In reality you see nothing, for the bat is a blur. These photographs suspend each

thousandth of a second for careful study. Photographs that unfortunately do not exist of Sisler, Cobb or Hornsby.

The secret weapon that helps Willie endure a season of continuous all-out effort and not collapse from exhaustion in August is the frivolity in his bloodstream. Many power hitters in baseball have had a case history of moodiness, which saps power under pressure. Willie Mays has doubled his strength with laughter.

The Man

Stanley Frank Musial was a baseball player from Donora, Pennsylvania. They called him Stan the Man. He played in the National League for twenty-two years as a St. Louis Cardinal outfielder-first baseman, from 1941 to 1963. (This is the way a father will tell it to his son in years to come.) For twenty-one consecutive years he played in a hundred or more games, and for seventeen of those years he hit over .300. He played in 3,026 games. He came up to the plate and wiggled and jiggled and swung the bat in a lazy arc, coiled and set for the pitch 10,972 times, hitting the ball safely 3,630 times and crossing the plate 1,949 times for St. Louis—all records in the league! His lifetime batting average was .331, and in one out of every three years he played he won the batting crown. His seven championships: 1943, .357; 1946, .365; 1948, .376; 1950, .346; 1951, .355; 1952, .336; 1957, .351. He led the league in long hits seven years and had 1,377 that were not singles—725 doubles, 177 triples, 475 home runs!

He led the league in most two-base hits for eight years, hitting fifty or more three seasons. He led five years for triples, six years in most base hits. In 1946 he led in eight batting categories. He got 2,504 extra bases on long hits and led the league in most total bases 13 seasons, 10 consecutively—his lifetime total was 6,134. He batted in a hundred or more runs in ten seasons for a career total of 1,951.

But with all Stanley's achievements on the diamond my dearest friend George Sisler phrased the most fitting tribute when he said, "I judge a ballplayer not in what era he plays or who he plays against but how he plays the game. Stan Musial would have been a great hitter in any era. I was more interested in the game of baseball and playing it well than in what I would get out of it. He is too. His interest and devotion to the game come first, and this is why he has played so long and so consistently well to establish his records. But his greatest contribution is not in the record book, and this is his character and the credit the man has been to baseball—the fine example he has set for men and boys all over our country."

Stan Musial was the most-liked player in the league. He would hit everywhere, but in Ebbets Field he would hit especially well. It was said that Musial owned Ebbets Field. When he coiled for the pitcher's delivery with Roy Campanella behind the plate for Brooklyn and then stepped into a pitch, it was a double in the alley or a quick goodbye over the wire-screen fence into Bedford Avenue. The faithful in Flatbush will always remember him at that moment *(next page)*.

The Pitchers

FOR SIXTEEN YEARS in the majors, beginning in 1871, the official rules permitted a batter to call out to the pitcher from his position in the batter's box for the pitch he wanted—high or low. Things have changed! Can you picture Harmon Killebrew calling out to Whitey Ford and asking for a belt-high pitch? Or with two men on and the score tied, Henry Aaron facing the great curve-ball pitcher Sal Maglie *(at left)*, motioning with his hands across the letters and yelling above the crowd, "Put it right here"? I can imagine where Mr. Maglie would have put it.

In 1879 a pitcher was allowed to throw nine balls before a batter took first base. Ten years later it was reduced to four and has remained so ever since. In 1963 the strike zone, that area above the width of the plate, was increased from the knees to the batter's shoulders instead of his armpits.

During the past seventy years, however, the art of pitching has remained pretty much the same. The batter does not know what is coming, and when the ball gets to the plate the pitcher intends it to pass through the strike zone in such a way that it will be unhittable. Pitching is an art, and like many others it takes a young man years of learning to acquire effective pitching knowledge and skills.

There are three kinds of pitchers in the major leagues. The first kind gives the batsman a problem with stuff. He makes it hard to get the bat and ball middles together. He is a problem in the vertical zone—an imaginary one erected immediately in front of the plate. He is a speedster, a strikeout artist. He has stuff, managers call it. His name could be Walter Johnson. He doesn't need a screwball, a slow curve, a change of pace or a slider. Walter Johnson was not a pitcher in the generally accepted sense of the word. He was a thrower. All he had to do was rear back and throw the ball through the middle, and not often could the batter hit it squarely. This is one class of major-league pitcher: the Amos Rusies, the Cy Youngs, the Guy Bushes, the Ed Walshes, the Smoky Joe Woods, the Rube Waddells, the Lefty Groves, and many others over the years.

The second class are pitchers and not throwers. They need superb control and they are expert in varying velocity. A batsman anticipates a certain speed, starts his swing, but finds that the ball is not yet up to the plate. The next pitch gives the illusion of great speed in contrast to the previous one and is met well back of the plate. This kind of pitcher has changes of speed, perhaps two curves, a slider, a change-up off the first ball, or a dipsy-do (the old time parabola slow ball). This sort of pitcher also makes good in the majors: Carl Hubbell, Preacher Roe, Sal Maglie, Ed Lopat, Robin Roberts, Bobby Shantz and many others.

The third group is simply a combination of the first two, and all pitchers of the present era try to belong to this class. They afford a hitting problem in both zones, the vertical and horizontal. They may approach the Johnson fast ball and the Hubbell changes. They include such pitchers as Christy Mathewson, Grover Alexander, Dizzy Dean, Bob Feller, Kid Nichols, Jack Coombs, Burleigh Grimes, Eddie Plank, Whitey Ford, and Warren Spahn, and, of course, many others. The really great pitchers largely belong to this third group.

The Pitch

A COMBINATION of three factors determines the variables of all pitches. The first is velocity. The second is direction of the spin of the ball, and the third is the speed of the spin. A fourth is sometimes added by some college coaches (who as a class are more informed and more pedagogically able than most professional managers), namely, angle of delivery. Leaving out the angle of delivery, all pitches or variables of whatever kind depend on and are produced by the relationship of any one of the three to either of the others or indeed to both of the others. Changes in velocity with the same spin direction can give the change-up off the fast ball. The same effort for velocities, combined with different spin directions, will give the fast ball and the curves. The same effort for velocity with changes in both spin speed and spin direction gives fadeaways or sliders. The same effort for velocity and no defined spin direction or indeed none at all may, by intent, produce knuckle balls. If then the speed of the spin and its direction are combined with changes of velocities, obviously different pitches are effected and a myriad of them are produced.

A prominent engineer of the General Electric Company who was measuring pitching speeds in my training camp told me that no human being could reproduce any previous pitch with electronic sameness however he tried. If the pitcher is deceptive with the unavoidable variations of the same pitch, pity the poor batter when he faces intentional variations both in deflection and velocities with a round ball and a round piece of wood.

The coaching of a pitcher, particularly as he acquires new pitches, challenges him to employ with his muscles what his understanding of instruction tells him to do. There are a number of aptitude tests that are used in workouts with young pitchers. Some boys are hopelessly slow in learning a new pitch. In those exceptional cases, the coach tells the youngster (in acquiring a change-up, for example), "Place the ball in your hand exactly as you throw your fast ball. At the finish of your delivery, loosen up on the pressure of your fingertips." A Brecheen or a Drysdale will produce all manner of pitches simply by suggestion. A Dizzy Dean will do it on his own. Generally speaking, results depend upon the amount of work on the part of the pitcher, but, of course, physical ability is a limiting factor. In some cases overwork may result in a sore arm or a strained tendon. Most coaching of pitchers is best done not by command but by fertile suggestion. Never try to *make* a

boy acquire a new pitch. A young pitcher must want to extend his repertoire on his own.

Although a pitcher can win in the major leagues if he knows only two pitches, all pitchers should acquire a third usable pitch, a change-up, or a slow curve, slider or a knuckler, thrown with the same delivery with which he throws his fast and curve balls. It helps the great pitcher and saves the career of the otherwise ordinary pitcher.

In the last half-dozen years or so the slider has become a popular pitch. Generally speaking I don't like the slider. I don't believe in it. The slider devalues more pitchers than it helps. It is a comparatively easy pitch to learn. Therefore I say without fear of contradiction from most major-league managers that the slider has precarious value. I think it is unfortunate that young pitchers seem to feel that the slider must be necessary in their bag of pitches. More assiduous application to the improvement of the curve or concentration on control or acquiring a usable change-of-pace pitch off either the fast ball or the curve, or both, would bring the pitcher to the major leagues more quickly and more permanently.

When a good curve ball breaks, it is quite a thing to see. A pitcher who throws one has the knack of combining the optimum velocity of a baseball with the optimum rotation. This art over a distance of sixty feet, six inches—pitcher's rubber to home plate—will produce the maximum curve. If you change the velocity-rotation combination you change the curve.

There are two decidedly different curve-ball pitches. The rainbow, jug handle, or round house curve is slow and breaks up to three or four feet. The quick breaking curve that baseball men refer to as dropping off the edge of the table is a strike-out pitch. Clem Labine, Johnny Sain, and Johnny Vander Meer had both of these. The curve is a great variable because one pitcher will have velocity so adjusted to the rate of rotation that the measurements are never the same as the curve-ball measurements of some other pitcher. In fact, if you change anything in the field of causes you change the curve.

The fast ball is released so that there is a back-spin. Pressure is applied down with the forefinger and middle finger: the bottom of the ball spins up to cause a rising fast ball (one that is live or takes off) when it is thrown overhand. If thrown three-quarters arm by a right-hand pitcher, the ball will move up and into a right-handed batter. A sinking fast ball from a right hander will break down and in. The curves of a southpaw will naturally move in an opposite arc across the plate.

The curve is thrown with even finger pressure and various finger grips depending on the kind of curve, but the idea is to twist the wrist or break it in a downward motion so that the ball comes over the top of the index finger *(see hand in picture at top right)*. This puts front spin on the ball, causing the top of the ball to spin downward.

The slider is a combination of fast-ball speed and partial curve-ball spin, but the wrist doesn't break *(picture lower right)*, the two fingers point ahead, and there is pressure on the middle finger as the ball is released. The *middle finger* is the key finger in a pitcher's delivery. Of course there will be variations in the effect of the slider depending on the pitcher. One pitcher may break the wrists *imperceptibly* in throwing the slider. They say seventy miles per hour is the speed for the optimum curve, but a slider is thrown faster. Because the wrist doesn't break, the ball has less rotation on leaving the hand. The rotation is more rapid with some, less rapid with others. The velocity is greater, but the slider's deflection from the straight line of the fast ball is less by far than the curve ball because a slider breaks so late in flight. In changing the velocity-rotation balance the pitcher is causing the forces of air pressure during the flight of the ball to take effect at a different time.

Don Newcombe has been publicized as the daddy of the pitch now commonly called a slider. His was a velocity pitch (hard to differentiate at times from his fast ball) which slid from the line of a fast ball in the direction of a curve. It was very effective. But it was Newcombe's curve ball.

In the final analysis control is the prime requisite of a pitcher. If he has a great assortment of pitches and moves the ball around—pitching to spots as they say—it all depends on control. If he has all the natural *stuff* in the world he still must get the ball over the plate to get the most batters out and hold the opposition to a low-run total. In fact, the physical differences in each pitch will be enough to move it around.

The significant pitcher's statistic ERA means Earned Run Average. ERA reflects the number of earned runs a pitcher allows per nine-inning game. If Whitey Ford pitches nine innings and wins 2-1, the run against him being earned, he has obviously an ERA of 1.00 for that game. Had he pitched only three innings and allowed an earned run, you would multiply the one earned run by 9 (innings in a game) and divide by 3 (innings he pitched) for an ERA of 3.00. One-third innings are dropped and two-thirds innings pitched are counted as total innings. The pitcher's ERA on a season is a reliable indicator of his value.

Night and Day

There is an inescapable point behind the fact that seven men hit .400 twelve times between 1900 and the advent of night baseball in 1935 and one man hit .400 since night baseball. Night games alone are the strongest single reason for the extinction of the .400 hitter. When Ted Williams hit .406 in 1941 the entire American League played only 35 night games. In 1950, 16 teams played 392 night games and 6 men hit over .325. In 1963, 20 teams played 862 night contests and *one* player hit over .325.

Great pitching will dominate any game, but at night the pitcher has an added advantage because the contrast of light changes a hitter's depth perception.

Both Sandy Koufax of Los Angeles *(left)* and Warren Spahn of Milwaukee *(right)* are great left-handed pitchers. Whitey Ford *(previous page)* is another. Ford, along with Dizzy Dean, is pitch for pitch perhaps the best one-game pitcher of all time. But Ford's earned-run average over eleven years is an incredible 2.78. Spahn looks the same on every pitch, in control of himself and the situation. The picture at right was taken on a Sunday afternoon —his 40th birthday. In 1963, at the age of 42, he ripened with a 23-7 record, a 2.60 ERA, twenty-two complete games, and seven shutouts. As Stan Musial said, "I don't think Spahn will ever get into the Hall of Fame. He'll never stop pitching."

Sandy Koufax has pitched two no-hitters and struck out eighteen batters in one game, thirty-one in two consecutive games, and 306 in a season. He pitched eleven shutouts in 1963 while winning twenty-five games, with an ERA of 1.88.

In these two portraits both pitchers look intently for the sign. Spahn, completely relaxed, with his big fielder's glove and the ball held behind his hip, sets his jaw as he looks to his catcher, Del Crandall. Sandy Koufax, leaning in, the ball shielded in his glove in front of him, strains to see John Roseboro's guarded signal in the night shadows. The signs are given by the catcher with the right hand held against the inside of the right thigh. The pitcher watches the full series of finger signals, including the decoy signs, before he begins his motion. This is especially important with second base occupied to prevent the runner from picking off a sign and then with a gesture of his own relaying a tipoff to the batter. If Koufax declines the catcher's first sign he will flick his glove. Spahn will shake off a sign or accept it with a slight turn of the head. Agreed on the pitch, the catcher sets in his crouch and forms a target with his mitt as the pitcher's windup begins.

Ball is a blur until on top of hitter *(top right)* as Koufax conceals pitch for stretch, kick and throw in full overhand motion.

Spahn swings arms back, kicks high, drops left arm down and throws. Ball is seen by batter from moment it leaves his hand *(below)*.

Pick-Off Move

Pitchers need to and ought to have more baseball knowledge and mastery of numerous skills than any other position player in the game—and when I make that statement I accept debate with any one or all of the catchers.

More important to the pitcher than to any other

position is the handling of emotions. He should display none. No momentary exaltation, no depressive thinking, no fear, no anger, no sudden flurry of overconfidence ending in carelessness, no slight disturbance by a base runner of his continuous concentration on the batsman—none of these must affect the isolated effectiveness of every single pitch.

In addition, he should be a finished professional in the art of holding men on bases, all bases, including the third one. This sequence of pictures presents the prize possession and value of the art of the "pick-off" at first base.

At first base, there are many times when the stolen base is decisive, universally expected, and managerially ordered. In a late inning, with a tie score and a capable base stealer on first and a dangerous hitter at bat, the "steal" is in order. It is then of immediate importance that the pitcher "hold the runner!"

The right-hand pitcher's most prevailing fault is imbalance of his weight. The inexperienced pitcher (and many in the majors) bears 90% of his body weight on the pivot foot. Overweight on the pivot foot *means shoulder movement tip-off to the base runner.* Many managers, particularly the young ones—major, minor, or amateur—need to know that the first corrective measure to be taken

is to see that the pitcher distributes his weight on both feet. Other suggestions on the pick-off move are in order to right-hand pitchers, but I shall mention only one: viz., a right-hand pitcher should start his pitch on the pick-off in advance of his step. That is not easy to do. This instruction is sometimes best understood by the pitcher if he is told to throw to first without stepping at all. The pitcher immediately finds out that he cannot follow that instruction, but it does get into his thinking that

he must start his arm or hand movement simultaneously with the start of his step, or preferably, in advance of it.

The left-hander is facing first base and so does not throw across his body. The marvelous lesson for left-hand pitchers—showing the exact physical movement of a left-hand pitcher in holding men on first base—is shown here by Warren Spahn.

First let it be said that any left-hand pitcher who allows a big lead or the advantageous break to the base runner is either grossly stupid or doesn't care enough, or both. Because the left-hander has command of the base runner, he is in the position to say, "Heads I win, tails you lose." If the runner breaks, he is caught off. If he does not break, there is no stolen base. Over the years many left-hand pitchers were masters of the runners on first base —Warren Spahn, Whitey Ford, Nick Altrock of yore, Sherrod Smith of Brooklyn's ancient days.

In this sequence of pictures we see the key to Spahn's pick-off technique. In picture 1 (top left), he is in his set position with his left foot on the pitching rubber carefully watching the runner on first base. The second picture shows the fraction of a second when Spahn, in the middle of his famous high right-leg kick, initiates the pitching step.

This is not simply a presentation of one pitcher

who has great aptitude and exceptional ability—it is a universal lesson to left-hand pitchers in holding men on first base. The key of the six pictures is picture 2. It shows the exact learning point for every prospective left-hand pitcher. At the position in picture 2, Spahn can go to the right as in picture 5, and then to picture 6 for the pick-off throw. Or, from 2 he can go to 3, where he is then committed to the plate pitch, and then go on to the finish of delivery in picture 4.

The key to the left-hand pitcher's artistry, I repeat, is in picture 2, where the "pause" comes into play. It is the delicate timing, may I call it, of holding the knee for a fraction of a second in almost complete stoppage at its high point in the kick. Naturally, if the pitcher chooses, he may not stop at all, and frequently he doesn't. In between comes the subtle pause, and it is just that. In picture 2, Spahn can go instantly and with full force in either direction to first, or on through to the plate. If the runner is breaking, he is a goner. Jackie Robinson, one of the best, was caught off twice in one game by Warren Spahn.

Several minor deceptions can be added, including head movements. A pitcher with spot control can look directly toward the base runner at the "pause" point in picture 2, and still pitch to the desired spot at the plate. Spahn's head position in this picture, however, seems to be at the halfway position. It permits by indirect vision the observation of the base runner's break, or body-leaning, as it is called. Picture 2 shows the usual head position, but it can be varied.

The point of the whole mastery of this pitching art is in the sliding scale of the pause. The base runner not only loses his intention to attack, but after a few throws he is reduced to complete surrender of any intent to attack. He becomes a private soldier in the army of safety first.

Intelligent and ambitious left-hand pitchers can become highly successful gamblers in the subtlety of the pause, just as Spahn and others have.

Now and then, but not often, such pitchers are outguessed by the base runner, who may occasionally divine that the pitcher is not going to pause at all, but will pitch to the batsman in a continuous wind-up and delivery. He breaks and wins. On those occasions the pitcher, who doubtless has paid little or no attention to the base runner, regrets he did not pause at the high point of his right knee. Some left-hand pitchers do not have the wind-up move or the high-kick move with the right knee that permits the pause. There have been and there are now some left-hand pitchers whose delivery does not permit the pause and they deliver without any preliminary delay, and they are quick enough to be effective.

Young Pitchers and the Staff

A pitcher with fine control and the extra pitch is a good young pitcher. Bill Monbouquette of Boston *(above left)* has the best slider. From the bench you cannot differentiate it from his fast ball. Juan Marichal of San Francisco *(center)* is brilliant with speed, curves, and a change. Steve Barber *(right)* has a fast ball that travels at ninety-six miles per hour, so he gets by without much of a curve. His fast ball breaks down and into a left-handed batter, and his slider breaks into a right-hander. He's known as a low-ball pitcher and allows very few home runs. Al Downing and Jim Bouton of the Yankees, Gary Peters of the White Sox, Jim Maloney and Jim O'Toole *(overleaf)* of Cincinnati, Culp, Bennett, Art Mahaffey and Jim Bunning *(opposite page)* of Philadelphia, and Dick Calmus of the Dodgers should win in the sixties.

If the effectiveness of scouting, coaching, trades, and work bring a number of young pitchers to-gether on one club in the same year to comple-ment a veteran pitcher, a strong staff is created and the life of the club is assured. The 1914 Miracle Braves of George Stallings beat Mr. Mack's power-ful club in the Series with George Tyler, Bill James, and Dick Rudolph, and in 1963, Koufax, Podres, and Drysdale snuffed out the Yankees in four straight. And so it has been in the years between. The pitching staff is the heart of the team.

Cleveland's big three *(below)* in the mid-fifties were such a staff. Joining the incomparable Bob Feller near the end of his career, twenty-game win-ners Early Wynn, Bob Lemon, and Mike Garcia won a total of 512 games for Cleveland and most of the Indians' record 111 wins in 1954. An argument could be made that the New York staff of Reynolds, Raschi, Lopat, and Ford was the best-balanced and strongest pitching staff in history, since in five straight World Series the Yankees were unbeatable.

"He's Got a No-Hitter Going…"

In this sequence of pictures the Boston pitcher has the Yankees on the hook. The scoreboard in the first picture *(top left)* shows it is the bottom of the seventh and there's a no-hitter going! Since the fifth inning the murmur has been going through the stands, the announcer has mentioned that he is not going to mention it, and on the Boston bench the superstitious players don't think about it. Suddenly with a two-and-two count the Yankee batter bounces a Baltimore chop high off the plate, and in the next four frustrating pictures the pitcher waits for it to come down. Too late, the ball is off his glove, the runner is safe. The no-hitter is gone. The pitcher relaxes, there is a mental adjustment, a change. The next batter hits the first pitch to the bleacher wall for a triple. A big inning. The shower —for a pitcher who just had a no-hitter going.

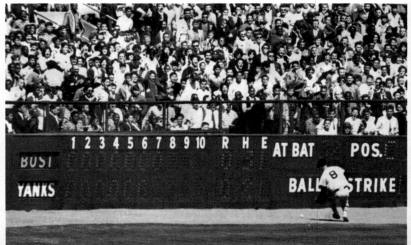

Relief from the Bullpen

Joe Page of the Yankees and Jim Konstanty of Philadelphia began the new era of the tireless relief specialist, the pitcher who could pitch every day and save a game if the starting pitcher failed. Both men helped win pennants, and now ace relievers, the most vital part of a contending team's bench, and pennants are synonymous. Konstanty appeared in seventy-four of the 154 games his team played in 1950 and then started the World Series. Joe Black of the Dodgers, Don Mossi with Cleveland, Hoyt Wilhelm with the Giants (below right, with his knuckler) pitched in a decade of television when the relief pitchers became nationally known, receiving salaries of $25,000 a year or more. As the sixties began, four pennants were won primarily by the key man in the bullpen: Elroy Face (below left), who after an 18-1 record in 1959 won ten for Pittsburgh in 1960, Jim Brosnan for Cincinnati and Luis Arroyo for New York in 1961, and Ron Perranoski for the Dodgers in 1963. The future trend of major-league clubs will see the development of relief specialists in the minors—not like the old days, when relievers were tired veteran pitchers on the way out.

High and Inside

The high fast inside pitch is a purpose pitch. It is the strikeout pitch of all ages. After you set up a batter by working around the area of the strike zone, high and inside is the strikeout pitch. But I don't think there is a pitcher in all of baseball who voluntarily and intentionally throws at a batter's head with the full intention of hitting him in the head. And furthermore, no one in the history of baseball has ever been hit on the head by a pitch that was thrown as high as a batter's head when he is set in the batter's box. When a batter takes his stride into a pitch, his head moves lower. The Carl Mays pitch that hit Chapman and killed him was chest-high.

No manager can want to hit a batsman. It defeats his purpose. That puts a man on base when a manager wants to get him out. I think I know Leo Durocher as well as anybody in this country, and although he might talk it up for effect in the give-and-take tactics on the field, I don't believe that he or any manager ever really wanted to hit a batter.

An Eye for an Eye

Anger, frankly, is the biggest enemy a pitcher has. It is an inexcusable affliction. Anger affects the delicate workings of a great pitcher in a close ball game. No constructive thought can come out of anger. The pitcher will lose control of the ball as soon as he loses control of himself. It happens suddenly, an umpire's call on a three-and-two pitch perhaps, and then you see it. You see it on Don Drysdale's face *(at left)*. An Ernie Broglio or a Steve Barber will succumb to it. There is panic on the bench. You just hope somebody will lose a shoe so you can call time while the pitcher settles. A manager rushes out to try to divert his attention.

A man who is master of himself in other ways will master himself on the mound. Mathewson, Alexander, or, today, Vernon Law have never showed their feelings.

Above we see the pitcher's nemesis—the line drive through the box. But there is no reciprocal idea here. Very few batters can intentionally hit a ball right at the pitcher. The picture at left shows Drysdale instinctively, in a fraction of a second, raise his glove to his head to catch a wicked line drive from Willie McCovey's bat. Drysdale yanks his head, the ball is in the webbing, McCovey's right foot has not even moved. At right the six-foot-five, 220-pound pitcher is knocked to the ground from the impact of the drive, but holds the ball.

The Umpire

The umpire in chief shall stand behind the catcher; take full charge and be responsible for the proper conduct of the game; call and count balls and strikes; call and declare fair balls and fouls; make all decisions on the batter; inform the official scorer of the official batting order and any changes in the lineups; announce any special ground rules *(below)*; start the game and stop the game by calling time; postpone the game because of weather; decide on a time limit for concluding it; and if necessary decide when a game shall be forfeited. Each umpire on the field has authority to disqualify any player, coach, or manager for objecting to decisions or for unsportsmanlike conduct or language and to remove them from the game and the field. Any umpire's decision that involves judgment is *final*. No player, coach, or manager shall object to such judgment decisions. No umpire shall criticize, seek to reverse, or interfere with another umpire's decision, and no umpire shall be replaced unless he is injured or becomes ill. Each umpire is the representative of the league and of professional baseball and is authorized and required to enforce all of these rules.

Where do you find such a man?

A man involved in a game who has the authority of a sea captain, the discretion of a judge, the strength of an athlete, the eye of a hunter, the courage of a soldier, the patience of a saint, and the stoicism to withstand the abuse of the grandstand, the tension of an extra-inning game, the invective of a player, and the pain of a foul tip in the throat.

He must be a tough character, with endurance and the ability to keep his temper and self-control, he must be unimpeachably honest, courteous, impartial, and firm, and he must compel respect from everyone! Hank Soar *(left)*, is such a man. He was a fine halfback with the Giants. Cal Hubbard was another of the great pros, a tackle in the football Hall of Fame and now head of the American League umpires. Al Barlick and Beans Reardon, Pinelli and Donatelli, McGowan and Conlan, Magerkurth and Summers, Connolly and Rigler, O'Day, Billy Evans, and, of course, Bill Klem.

The umpire forgets which is the home or visiting club, which player called him names the night before, who the super star or the unknown pinch hitter is. The players are faceless. The play's the thing. The umpire keeps his eye everlastingly on the ball. His position is vital, his angle of vision is the key. He is on top of it, because he knows a player will question a decision if he is out of position to see it clearly. From the upper deck the fan sees the tie-breaking run for the visiting team slide home and sees his outfielder make a perfect throw and the catcher block the plate for the tag and he's out. Safe? What? Is that ump crazy? In the dust the umpire sees only the ball *(next page)*.

The Long, Hot Summer

Sometimes during a double-header in St. Louis, Cincinnati or Baltimore the temperature goes over a hundred. The umpire's dark suit holds the sun's heat and his face is covered by the binding, heavy steel and leather mask. Under his coat he wears the shoulder pads connected to the steel ribbed chest protector. There are shin guards like a catcher's under his pants and steel plates over his shoes. He holds a crouch on every pitch, never leaves the plate to sit in the shade of the dugout for half innings. Although the pay and the hours are good and there are only twenty umpires in each league and fifteen thousand in the bushes who would like his job, sometimes he must wonder about the job.

There is much less arguing on the field now than there was fifty years ago. There wasn't a game played then when you did not see heated arguments. It does not mean if you do not object or argue that you don't want to win. Nor is the opposite true. Leo Durocher has a loud clear voice and a sharp pointed finger, and he enjoys a good rhubarb. In the pictures above, Los Angeles' manager can't get in a word as Leo and the ump tell each other off, and the fans enjoy the tantrum, though they cannot hear a word. Below are the faces of the men spewing fire from their mouths, because they *know* absolutely and unequivocally that they are right and that the umpire blew it. Although he does make mistakes, the major-league umpire is the finest field official in any sport, is *usually* right, and *always* wins. In any event, it should be and *is* gratifying to all good sportsmen in this country that we are approaching the British standard of the acceptance of field discipline.

The Catchers

I was a catcher. I liked to hit and was proud of my throwing arm—in fact, that got me into the major leagues. Then an off-season injury cut short my career after the 1905, 1906, and 1907 seasons. It was in the gym of the University of Michigan, where I was coaching the baseball team during the winter. I was not warmed up one day and I seriously injured my arm demonstrating throwing technique. I had the good fortune to remain in baseball as a manager. After his playing days are over an intelligent catcher should be well qualified for advancement to scouting or managership. Mr. Mack, Mickey Cochrane, Paul Richards, Birdie Tebbetts, Al Lopez and now Mr. Berra are some of the top receivers who prospered after catching.

A clear indication of a catcher's exceptional intelligence is his social gift of engaging in enlightened conversation with batsmen while behind the plate. The great Gabby Hartnett had it, Campanella had it, Berra had it, and Bill Delancey, my young catcher of thirty years ago, was highly proficient in the art. If the catcher can place in the batter's mind the slightest suggestion that he must select one out of two or more prospective pitches in the next delivery, he has made a guess hitter out of the batsman. The veteran hitter pays no attention to conversation, but with many—and not always the youngster—talking a pitcher's stuff and its variances gets results.

How well I remember when I returned to the St. Louis Browns in Philadelphia in 1906. I had been home for several days on account of the illness of my mother, and I was catching the first day after my return. When I came to bat in the second inning, Ossie Schreckengost, the famous catcher for the Philadelphia Athletics, spoke kindly to me, calling me by first name. "When did you get back, Branch?" I was pleased with the old catcher's inquiry, and I said, "Just this morning, Ossie." The call was two and two when he said to me, "You have been to see your mother, haven't you?" I said, "Yes, I have," but I didn't turn toward him. Then he said, "How is she, Branch?" I turned to look at the old fellow squatting so low behind me and I said, "She is better, thank you." When I looked up, Chief Bender had started his pitch. I froze and took the strike dead through the middle. "Ha, ha," said Schreck. You could have heard him in the outfield. "Ha, ha," said he, "I struck you out." So he had.

Yogi and Campy

In the last decade the two dominant catchers in baseball were Roy Campanella of Brooklyn *(pages 156-157)* and L. P. Yogi Berra *(here)* of the New York Yankees. By 1955 they were at the top of their game, and each had earned the Most Valuable Player award in his respective league for the third time. Both men were clutch hitters with extra-base power, both were deceptively fast for their short, stocky physiques, both were very smart behind the plate. Campanella was an artful glove man, a master at handling the low pitch, and both Campy and Yogi had splendid throwing arms. Campanella would rifle the ball to any base without taking a step. They have hit over 550 home runs between them, surpassing all catchers in history in this department. No one, it seems, will ever equal Yogi Berra's record of fourteen All-Star games or his record of seventy-five games in fourteen World Series. Can you imagine, Berra has played *half a regular season in the World Series!* Baseball may never see two such talented men for a long time.

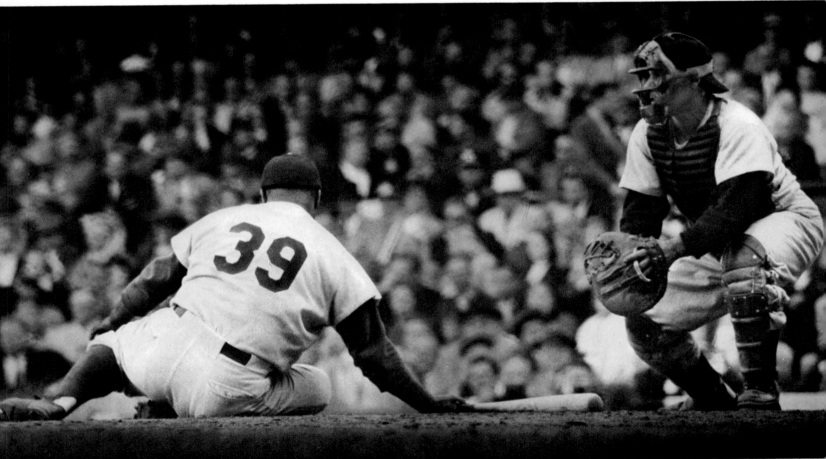

It may be a mark of respect for a receiver's batting ability when a catcher calls for a tight pitch. Here Yogi sits Campy down.

Young Catchers

You cannot win a pennant with a poor catcher. And how often the best catcher in baseball is in the World Series! A pennant winner must be strong *everywhere,* and this strength starts behind the plate. They say you can't win a flag with a kid catcher, but the Cincinnati Reds did it in 1961 with youthful Johnny Edwards *(right)* and the Cardinals in 1964 with Tim McCarver. The San Francisco Giants became solid contenders when their great young catcher Tom Haller *(left)* came up to take over the job. Everything about him is perfection. He is one of the finest young catchers I've ever seen. Great from the beginning. His coach, Wes Westrum, who was an excellent defensive catcher with the Giants, agrees. "Like Earl Battey of Minnesota he is a big man who can do everything. Indestructible." One factor in favor of the young catchers today, Westrum will tell you, is the oversized catcher's mitt *(below).* "During my ten years with the Giants I had ten broken fingers and an uncountable number of split nails. Besides, the pain of a damaged finger impairs a catcher's ability to grip the ball and especially the bat, and he loses valuable time out of action, which is dangerous to a club in a close race. The big glove does eliminate some passed balls, but practically all damaged fingers are caused by foul tips. Don't I know! In my two years I broke three fingers—but in those days you continued to play!"

THE FIRST qualification of a major-league catcher is a strong throwing arm—strong enough to throw to second base without "running with the ball." The catcher must move his left foot and throw on the right footstep. He should not add any more steps. He must throw a straight ball with the spin directly back toward himself so that the ball does not sail out to the right.

Whenever and wherever he catches the ball, he should bring his throwing hand instantly to the throwing position. There must be no windup in a catcher's throw. It is an angular movement to throw quickly.

He must know what it means to shift, not as a cross movement of one foot past the other, but as a double movement with one foot moved to the other, both really moving almost at the same time. He can thereby reduce the number of wild pitches. It is a safe statement to say that fewer than half the catchers in the major leagues have learned to shift.

Body checking should be the habitual practice of every catcher. Little League catchers can body check, and most do. It's a simple matter to drop to the knees in a blocking effort on all dirt pitches with a runner on base anywhere. There must be no chance taking as if he were a shortstop.

The catcher seldom has an excuse for the low-pitched fast ball getting by him. In fact, any passed ball is a grievous error and should be taken into consideration in judging the defensive ability of a receiver. A passed-ball catcher is not a catcher.

A catcher must be nimble with catlike reflexes to pounce on a bunt, spin after a pop fly, or dive for the tag after an errant throw to the plate, as Elston Howard does (top left) at a runner who does not slide. Most of all the catcher needs strength and stamina to block the plate from the runner coming in to score. How well he guards it with his left foot and how well he braces for the collision and how quick he is at putting the tag on the runner and holding the ball is the show-down test that decides many a ball game. The toughest tag for a catcher is on the throw from the right-field line when the runner comes into his blind side and arrives at the same instant as the ball (below left). The catcher must block the plate, catch the ball, make the tag, and immediately check to keep the runners on base from advancing. The catcher who turns to argue a close call with runners on base has a lot to learn.

I have said that a strong arm is the first quali-fication of a catcher. That is assuming that the catcher can catch. The catcher who frequently muffs pitches, particularly when the runner at first base has broken for the steal, needs demotion. That is the very time when most catchers do drop the ball. Another very necessary quality of a good catcher is the ability to back up plays. On balls hit to the infield where the batsman is obviously out at first base, the catcher must extend himself. His running speed becomes important. It's a great asset if he is fast enough to retrieve a wild throw even as far as the near-right-field foul territory. A good catcher breaks as fast as the batsman himself and runs with just as much self-imposed purpose as the batsman. It is at this point that a cogent obser-vation is in order. You will see in the major leagues, day after day, catchers running to back up bases with their masks still in position. I can hardly imagine a boy in a foot race loading himself with two pounds of shot in a poke around his neck. He could do better with the shot than with a mask on his head, because the shot wouldn't bounce around all the time or interfere with his clear sight of where he was going. The mask can and fre-quently does. I have seen this very year a catcher actually chase a foul ball several times with his mask on. I am almost ashamed to admit that major-league catchers will run all over the place after passed balls and wild pitches—and back up on wild throws—with the mask decorating their undoubt-edly hard heads. It is a fine habit for a catcher to throw the mask on every touch of the ball by the bat. It becomes necessary to refer to it because of the continual violation of proper action.

Many catchers are accused of being dumb. Some inefficient pitching staffs are prone to think—and openly accuse—the catcher of not being correct in the calling of the pitch. It is the most inexcusable excuse for a pitcher that I know of. It is a self-indictment to make the charge, because the pitcher can always shake his head and get the pitch he wants. The pitcher is the final authority in deter-mining every pitch. True, the catcher can be very helpful, and he should come to know the hitting weaknesses of batsmen. He should be a scholarly student of hitters, really, with a fine memory of former games. I have known a number of catchers who kept book on hitters—noting the stage of the call, the pitch delivered and where thrown, and the results. Bill Delancey had this uncanny ability.

The catcher is in position to be the field general. He sees exactly where seven men are standing and he should be the master defensive tactician of the game. He should be able and willing not only to select the pitch but to indicate where it should go. It is a great day for a catcher when he comes to have sufficient confidence to assert himself in mov-ing this fielder or that, in or out or over, even to the point of stopping the game at a critical time and having a talk with the team captain or even the manager. A great catcher like Campanella or Cochrane or Delancey or Kling or Dickey practi-cally runs the game.

Brooklyn!

Some people are born here, some people come here, many people leave here, but all of them remember in different ways their days in Brooklyn.

This dark, gloomy, shrouded picture is a symbol of sadness for me and for hundreds of thousands of people. It shows the demolition of Ebbets Field, home of the Brooklyn Dodgers. The lamp-post reads Bedford Avenue and Sullivan Place, and over this historic spot in right field, Duke Snider often lost one, as did Stan Musial when he came to town. It is a bleak and empty place here in this last photograph. All the joy and love and great devotion have left this diamond behind the torn and tattered posters. The grandstand is leveled, the voices are silent. By some strange coincidence the picture was taken on the day, almost at the hour, that my son died. I lived in Brooklyn for eight years, but it doesn't take that long to fall in love with the place. I did. Branch Jr. did. Our whole family did. We were devoted to the people, the Dodgers and the ballpark.

Ebbets Field is now a memory, a lovable, cherished memory that only makes a Brooklynite regret that so-called progress or the prospects of private profit can so easily grieve the public trust. Brooklyn is a disappointed city. It has lost many of its landmarks of individuality. Its recreational personality is permanently hurt. *The Dodgers are gone.*

164

MY FAMILY was made up of Mrs. Rickey ("Mother" to all of us); five daughters, Mary, Jane, Alice, Sue, and Elizabeth; and one son, Branch Jr.

From his birth and for the next forty-seven years, Branch Jr. was my constant companion. He attended preparatory schools of my choosing. He graduated from my own alma mater, Ohio Wesleyan University. He attended my law school at the University of Michigan. He had no desire to become a lawyer. After two years I gave him the job of supervisor of minor-league clubs in the highly extended Cardinal organization in St. Louis. Within a year, Mr. Larry MacPhail, president of the Brooklyn club and surely baseball's soundest entrepreneur, asked me for Branch's services to handle his minor-league clubs. That was the most grievous decision I have ever faced. I finally agreed. Branch went to Brooklyn, and a couple of years later he was the inside and determinative reason for my going to Brooklyn.

My eight years in Brooklyn gave me a new vision of America, or rather America gave me a new vision of a part of itself, Brooklyn. They were wonderful years. A community of over 3,000,000 people, proud, hurt, jealous, seeking geographical, social and emotional status as a city apart and alone and sufficient—entirely distinct from the name "New York" or "Greater New York." Brooklyn as a town was older really than Manhattan. For always it had been a separate corporation, a selfish aspirant to distinction. Brooklyn was proud of the Brooklyn *Eagle,* the daily newspaper, and proud of its authors, painters, museum, and musicians.

As time went on, following the official incorporation of Brooklyn as a part of Greater New York, the Brooklyn Dodgers, its baseball club, became an honored proof of Brooklyn's identity among the cities of America. "We still exist as Brooklyn when the Dodgers take the field," said a prominent officer of the Brooklyn Trust Company. There was a deep sense of satisfaction when the Dodgers played the New York Giants. That was municipal equality. It was not only a jubilant artistic triumph when Brooklyn won, it was an expression of the composite personality of a people, who by the ardor of their support and the competitive superiority of their team had proved their independence from the giant municipal structure that had engulfed them. One could not live for eight years in Brooklyn and not catch its spirit of devotion to its baseball club, such as no other city in America equaled. Call it loyalty, and so it was.

It was a crime against a community of 3,000,000 people to move the Dodgers. Not that the move was unlawful, since people have the right to do as they please with their property. But a baseball club in any city in America is a quasi-public institution, and in Brooklyn the Dodgers were public without the quasi. Not even a succeeding generation will forget or forgive the removal of its Dodger team.

Oh, my, what a team they were! The one that developed and improved after the war and in the early fifties and finally won the world championship in 1955 for the first time in Brooklyn's history. This lineup will always be remembered, because they played together with little change in personnel for about eight seasons and were the first famous lineup to be seen nationally on television. The Dodgers were consistently exciting. Their range of player personalities and their excellence of play endeared them to millions of fans.

Every manager studies the order in which his nine men will hit before a season and before every game, having chiefly in mind the adaptation of a batsman's abilities to his position in the batting order, or lineup. His job is to produce full potential of scoring runs with this particular group of players in this particular park and against this particular opponent, primarily the opposing pitcher. His choice for a game is written on a card and presented to the plate umpire before the game begins. All men must bat in this prescribed rotation, and all pinch hitters must remain in the relative order.

There have been many great lineups over the years in baseball. Circumstance and history and the shrewd manipulation of the best managers and front-office brains every now and then brought a team of players together for a good number of years without change to form classic lineups. The 1927 Yankees had Earle Combs, cf, at leadoff, then Mark Koenig, ss, Babe Ruth, rf, Lou Gehrig, 1b, Bob Meusel, lf, Tony Lazzeri, 2b, Joe Dugan, 3b, and Benny Bengough, c. The 1930 Philadelphia Athletics lineup was legendary with Max Bishop, 2b, Mule Haas, cf, Mickey Cochrane, c, Al Simmons, lf, Jimmy Foxx, 1b, Bing Miller, rf, Jimmy Dykes, 3b, and Joe Boley, ss. My illustrious gashouse gang in St. Louis in 1934 brought Pepper Martin, 3b, Jack Rothrock, rf, Frank Frisch, 2b, Joe Medwick, lf, Ripper Collins, 1b, Bill Delancey, c, Earni Orsatti, cf, and Leo Durocher, ss, to the plate, followed by one of the Dean brothers.

There are those die-hard fans who will argue that the two lineups in the 1936 World Series were best known and most loved. The Yankees came to bat with a remarkable batting order: Frank Crosetti, ss, Red Rolfe, 3b, Joe DiMaggio, cf, Lou Gehrig, 1b, Bill Dickey, c, George Selkirk, rf, John Powell, lf, and Tony Lazzeri, 2b. The Giants had Joe Moore, lf, Dick Bartell, ss, Bill Terry, 1b, Hank Leiber, cf, Mel Ott, rf, Gus Mancuso, c, Burgess Whitehead, 2b, and Travis Jackson, 3b.

The photographs on these pages, beginning with Reese and Gilliam *(at right),* were taken at Ebbets Field during the 1955 World Series. This lineup may be the most famous of all, especially in the hearts of Brooklyn fans.

The loud-speaker in the ball park announces all the men in the lineup on their first appearance. The roars that followed each introduction of this Brooklyn team as they came to bat at Ebbets Field are gone now, but these pictures will bring their wondrous days on the diamond vividly to mind.

Batting first and playing shortstop, No. 1:
PEE WEE REESE

A leadoff hitter has only one job: to get on base. He must have a keen eye for balls and strikes. Reese once got on base three times in one inning! Pee Wee's fine legs and excellent judgment made him ideal at the top of the batting order, and his general mastery of batting skills made him ideal for second position as well. In percentage of number of steals per number of tries, Reese rates around the top. He is a fine example of a player who *learns* to hit from helpless nothing to acceptable something. Not many do. As captain of the team, Pee Wee Reese was outstanding in making the team integration of the Negro possible at Brooklyn.

Batting second and playing second base, No. 19:
JUNIOR GILLIAM

Here is a man who can adapt to any challenge: a switch hitter, left or right. He is a fine sample of a pro's pro. A superb bunter in every direction. Can pull or push the ball with intent right or left. He fits either first or second position in the batting order with a facility almost equal to that of Reese *(pictures previous page)*. Both are jealous of physical fitness. Both can run, throw, field, hit and think. When the marvelous Billy Cox retired as Brooklyn's third baseman, Robinson moved from second to third and Gilliam became the second baseman.

Batting third and playing center field, No. 4:
DUKE SNIDER

Power personified, the Duke had over 400 home runs in season play and eleven in the World Series! Great bat propulsion would cause him to miss many pitches, but his fine courage and physical coordination made him a power hitter to all fields. A strike swinging for the Duke was an awesome sight as he spun around and then jumped to regain his balance. He'd bring his right fist to his mouth and blow hot breath into it, then step back in and swing again from the heels *(at left)*. Batting left-handed he could fit any manager's picture in third,

fourth, or fifth position. Snider was splendidly placed in third position behind Reese, a right-hander, and Gilliam, a switch hitter. About the time that a left-handed pitcher would figure on striking out left-handed hitter Duke Snider, the next pitch would go over the fence.

The third, fourth, and fifth men in the lineup are always known as the heavy hitters—the meat! The fourth man bats cleanup, because with one stroke of his mighty bat a Foxx, a Gehrig, a Mantle, or a Musial could clean off a bases-loaded situation with a home run. One hit—four runs batted in. Someone, somewhere, one day decided that runs batted in were synonymous with power, a symbol of a great hitter. This runs-batted-in philosophy grew in popularity, and now RBI is a title of distinction, given great prominence in the press, on the radio and television, and in the published records of baseball itself. They are doubtless intended to be a comparative estimate of player values.

The insistence that the number of runs batted in denotes a basic standard for excellence is completely fallacious. I seldom look at the column in examining player records. Most major-league players, practically every one of them with any experience, will hit and do hit for the same batting percentage whether or not the bases are populated.

The one obvious weakness in estimating the worth of players by their number of RBIs is the tremendous difference in the dimensions of major-league ball parks. One player must play eighty-one games in his own park and only nine in another. It is 257 feet, let us say, to the right-field foul line in park number one, and a dead right-field hitter makes a great runs-batted-in record. In another park it is 350 feet to right field for a straightaway hitter. With the same number of times at bat, the straightaway hitter has many less runs batted in than the pull hitter. The park controls the RBI.

There is yet another feature that can work havoc on a player's RBI record and very often does. I will call that feature managerial control, and this is directly related to the lineup. The leadoff hitter is very fast and is a good base runner. He knows how to command a sizable lead and he is skilled and knowledgeable on the breaks. He draws many walks. He is always instructed, so it seems, to take, meaning not to strike at the next pitch. He has to take, and almost never does he get the chance to hit the cripple (an easy let-up pitch for the sake of the strike zone). He is needed as a base runner, another potential run. A better batsman is coming up with more power. Take, take, take—he is inured to it. He may be a Stanky and get 130 bases on balls in one season, but as a leadoff man, hit .275 and have very few runs batted in.

Batting fourth and playing third base, No. 42:

JACKIE ROBINSON

This rare photograph shows Jackie Robinson taking his little mincing steps in front of the catcher as he always did entering the box from the plate side. As a hitter he was good in any position from first to ninth. He seldom struck out and doubtless was one of the very best batsmen in the history of the game when the call included two strikes. Robinson was better under pressure. He could and did carry an extra load of hitting responsibility with grace, confidence and power. Robinson, like Snider, could fit the middle position in any batting order best, but if he batted first in an inning Jackie had the talent to drag a bunt past the pitcher and then steal all the way home.

Batting fifth and playing first base, No. 14:
GIL HODGES

You could not walk Robinson to bring up a slugger like Hodges. With one swing left, Gil was dangerous and unpredictable, and the runner on first was always in scoring position with Hodges at bat. He was never mindful of his own averages. The team came first. Hodges would be unaffected emotionally or in any other way wherever placed. He would step in with that ritual of his, spreading a big hand over the top of his batting helmet and pressing it firmly on his head, then picking at the shoulder seam of his shirt to loosen it, then swinging the bat out front. The fans were devoted to him, sticking with him in his slumps. He was a manager's pet without ever knowing it, and both would be mad if anyone thought so. He did not have the speed of the five men in front of him, but he had more speed than generally credited to him. He was an above-average major-league runner. Most of his 378 home runs were made against careful pitching, for the next batsman was just as dangerous.

This brings me to another factor: the batsman's position in the batting order and his RBI statistics. Obviously the leadoff man cannot drive in anybody in his first time at the plate. He starts off sorely handicapped for a runs-batted-in record. The second man cannot drive in more than one runner, and the first man, if on at all, is usually at first base, with 270 feet to go in order to score. The third man is much advantaged over the other two. Let us say he has power, maybe fifty per cent on sheer power rating (hits related to total bases). Therefore, half his hits average up to two-baggers. And the fourth man is even better placed for runs batted in than the third. He has three batsmen ahead of him with more chance for scoring runs. The fifth man probably (in most lineups) has the outstanding opportunity for runs batted in. Frequently a home-run hitter bats in the sixth position and is highly placed to impress the runs-batted-in devotees. Reverse two men in the hitting order and you will frequently reverse their RBI total.

It is shocking when club presidents and their general managers can be so gullible about RBI's. Most convincing are the many cases where a player hitting in the second place one year and in the fifth position another will show twice as many runs batted in. Surely it is valid evidence of thoughtlessness for baseball people to overstress the value of RBI's and thereby give the press and television a full right to spread the most misleading column of figures in baseball today.

Batting sixth and catching, No. 39:
ROY CAMPANELLA

Like Reese, he *learned* to hit. That means he showed remarkable improvement over his early days when he included head-high pitches as within the strike zone. He had power and rarely struck out swinging. Campy's wallop changed many a game, especially those thrilling Giant-Dodger clashes in the early fifties. He was always trouble at the plate as he held the bat by each end and snapped it behind his back to flex his shoulders before he hit. When he took a full cut his knee almost touched the dirt. He possessed a mixture of good fellowship and high combativeness fused in his very nature such as has never been exceeded in any player. And he could run! He will be in the Hall of Fame.

There is a final and more important criticism of the prevailing overemphasis on runs batted in, although Roy Campanella always ranked high in this department. I have already pointed out several reasons why RBI statistics are grossly misleading. But here is the clincher, and I deal with it convincingly, I hope, even to the laymen of the game.

As these veteran batsmen compress every advantage of their experience into the preparatory stance in the batter's box they lose sight of everybody and everything in the world except the pitcher. These veteran hitters, by sheer compulsion as well as by election, are concentrating wholly, completely, exclusively, *on the pitch,* and are unaffected by any outside or extraneous consideration or circumstance. At the final infinitely small split second preceding the pitch, a batter does not know whether the first baseman has moved closer or farther from first. He is thinking only of a good ball—a pitch within the strike zone—and has a firm desire to hit the ball with the bat in any direction—a fair ball, a safe hit. He is not thinking about the runner on second base any more than he is thinking about the picture show that night. I don't believe that any veteran batsman in baseball is generally affected one way or the other by the presence of a runner on first base or anywhere else.

The most realistic reason for criticism of the runs-batted-in records is the *aloneness* of the professional batsman when he faces the pitch. That reason lies deeper than and fully apart from the effects of the varying size of parks, or managerial controls, or placement in the batting order, or varying team batting abilities—all or indeed any one of which can and do change the runs-batted-in figures of all players.

Batting seventh and playing right field, No. 6:
CARL FURILLO

He could run and he had power at the plate, and I cannot quickly think of any outfielder who could outthrow him. He could qualify for a position higher up than seventh, but someone has to hit in the low positions, and Furillo in seventh place indicates a World Series team. It was said that he could be pitched to, and he could. Most batters, even the great ones, have so-called weaknesses. But about the time you had Carl struck out, he would deliver the unexpected line-drive base hit. Furillo possessed most of all an aggressive fighting spirit in the tradition of Slaughter or Bauer, and it won ball games.

Batting eighth and playing left field, No. 15:
SANDY AMOROS

Not very many clubs play 154 consecutive games with the same lineup. Injury, illness, staleness, slumps—something happens. And the team with adequate substitutes goes into the World Series. Amoros could run and throw and was not to be regarded as a fill-in. In this 1955 World Series his performance was sensational. With the series tied at three games apiece, Johnny Podres shut out the Yankees 2-0 in Yankee Stadium. Little Sandy made a game-saving run and catch on Yogi Berra's certain hit down the left-field line and turned it into a double play on a great relay from Reese to Hodges in the sixth inning to break a Yankee rally

Batting ninth and pitching, No. 17:

CARL ERSKINE

Erskine—pronounced "Oiskin" by some of the Flatbush fans—was a gentleman and a fine control pitcher with a consistent winning percentage. Carl pitched two no-hitters and struck out fourteen Yankee batters in the 1953 World Series.

The pitcher bats last in the majors usually because there are eight other men who can hit better than he can. The best hitters appear in the first five positions because they will come to bat more often and percentagewise over a season make more hits and score more runs. There are many times in college and sandlot baseball when the pitcher bats higher in the order, and frequently he is a fine hitter. In the majors the regular players are better batsmen, but on occasion a pitcher will be used as a pinch hitter, as Don Newcombe, the big Dodger pitcher, was on many occasions because of his extra-base power. Warren Spahn has hit over 33 home runs in his career, and Jim Tobin hit three consecutive home runs in one game for the Boston Braves in 1942. Pitchers will also be used to sacrifice with a bunt or a deep fly. Some pitchers cannot hit at all and bat less than .100 in a season, primarily because they don't work at it.

Geometry of the Diamond

The genius of fixing dimensions to accommodate the velocities of thrown and batted balls to the agility of human muscles and speed of legs resulted a hundred years ago in establishing the distances between bases at ninety feet. There has never been any suggestion to change those distances by anybody at any time. The infield single, the stolen base, the extra-base hit, the forced defensive position of infielders—all of these plays and many more could be cited as examples of the miraculous exactitudes involved in baseball. The umpire necessarily and unavoidably becomes simply the best guesser on the field. He violates the emotional judgment of 50,000 home fans in half of his decisions at second base on the steal and a fair percentage of the decisions at first base on infield hits. There is an uncanny, strangely appropriate relationship of distances and human physical effort. Another feature affecting this matter has to do with the resiliency of the ball, something Alexander Cartwright, who established the basic measurements of the diamond, had nothing to do with.

Setting the Infield

Managerial directives control placement of players *completely*. Placement depends on the manager's opinion of both his own and opposing players. There are certain standard placements to defend against the bunt.

The prearrangement of covering second base by the shortstop or second baseman on an anticipated hit-and-run play is first of all under managerial control. Usually, however, the decision is made by the second baseman or the shortstop, who consider the call of the pitch and the ability of the batsman to pull or push the ball.

Overshifting

Certainly there is great value in overshifting to accommodate batsmen who hit only to one field and don't know how to correct it. Cobb was always brashly outspoken in his criticism of Ted Williams. In Cobb's opinion, Williams needlessly permitted the defensive infield and outfield to shift to extreme right-field positions. Cobb believed Williams to be a great hitter with great power, but he always insisted that Williams should have kept the outfield and infield honest by hitting enough to the left side to keep all defensive players in their straightaway positions. Cobb believed that Williams could have learned it overnight. So do I.

Rundown

The rundown is possibly the most neglected defensive play in the game.

Let us say that the catcher has the ball with the runner trapped midway between third and home. The first thing the catcher does is to start toward the runner with all the speed he has, and instead of making the fake motion up high and above the waistline, he goes completely through with his arm swing. Basemen generally do not know the effect on the base runner of completely carrying through the fake throw. It brings the runner to a dead stop. The catcher's running speed increases instantly and frequently results in the catcher making the tag and never throwing the ball at all. When, in a major-league game, you see the ball thrown back and forth three or four times, you can very well know that the basemen don't know anything about how to catch the runner on a rundown. The full sweep of the arm on the part of a baseman is the key to the quick rundown and saves the play because the succeeding runner cannot advance as he would on a long rundown.

Another quick example of this rundown play presents itself when you find the pitcher in the middle of the diamond with the ball in his hands and a runner trapped completely between bases. Most pitchers in the major leagues will throw the ball to someone right away. He should start running, with all the speed he can command, directly at the base runner, making a complete follow-through with his arm, more than once if necessary, en route to his own tag. The soundness of this procedure is easily demonstrated with field practice.

Test Play

When managers say that a certain boy might be able to play second or third, but cannot play shortstop, they probably mean that he doesn't have the arm to make the play "in the hole." This play in the hole is frequently called the test play. The shortstop candidate, in normal position, must be able to go to his right on the hard-hit ground ball and shove his right leg out in full stride at the instant the ball hits his hands, thus putting him in position to throw the ball to first without moving the pivot foot—the right foot. If the player can do it one time, he can always do it. It is a bit difficult to describe the play with words but surprisingly easy to demonstrate it on the field. These pictures of Pee Wee Reese and Maury Wills show the play deep in the hole. There is, of course, a similar test play for the second baseman going to his right to get a ground ball and retire the runner at first.

Double Play

The defensive double play is the pitcher's savior. The infielders' positions are not determined simply on the basis of anticipating a double play. The inning, the score, the batsman's ability, the instructions to the pitcher on pitching to this particular batsman, and finally the batsman's ability both as to power and the direction of his hitting are all factors in determining the playing position of all four infielders and particularly the shortstop and the second baseman. All of these items are considered by shortstops like Phil Rizzutto, Al Dark, Pee Wee Reese, and Dick Groat in taking their pre-pitch positions. Dick's amazing coordination in quick starting largely accounts for his part in making record double plays, but his knowledge of his own pitcher and the probabilities of the pitch, together with a scholarly study of the opposing batsmen, permits Groat to have the justified reputation of being a smart infielder.

Five-Man Infield

The idea of the five-man infield would be sensational but I don't suppose it will be embraced in many years and yet it's reasonable to assume that major-league managers must give it consideration eventually.

It has been demonstrated in repeated trials at Vero Beach that a five-man infield is practical and sound and should be employed under some circumstances. Suppose the club afield has a one-run lead. It's a late inning and runners are on first and second with only one or none out. The pitcher is at bat. He is a good pitcher and cannot be lifted. He cannot hit a lick. His batting average year after year is less than .100. He strikes out when he swings. Good tactics would make the pitcher hit if it is at all possible. The defensive club really doesn't need *any* outfielder. So an outfielder is brought in and placed twenty-five feet from the home plate, ten feet in fair territory on the third-base side; the first baseman takes a similar position on the first-base side. This shift has two intents—first to make the weakling batsman *hit*, and second to get the second-base runner out on the force play at third. The shortstop holds the advance runner tight at second.

Andy High, an expert tactician and a major-league third baseman in his playing days, had charge of a battery of weak-hitting pitchers at this Vero Beach experiment. He would try to bunt, to drag, to use the sharp wrist snap calculated to pass by the two close fielders, or to hit straight away, as he might elect. The play was tried approximately 650 times, and the book shows that Andy upset the design only four times. Does any major-league manager or minor-league manager have the courage to try the play?

It is not conventional, but it works.

The unexpected tactics of John McGraw, who would have Pep Young steal on a fake bunt with nobody out, took advantage of surprise. McGraw had tactical guts, and this innovation, for it was just that, was much talked about over the years. Baseball is made up of too many hidebound, conservative tactics in the field of management.

It's a terrific thing, this timidity of managers. Oh, the rules of baseball are handled by conservative people. The genius of Alexander Cartwright is in the picture even today. The geometrical measurements have never been changed, but the positions of players have not been changed enough.

We approach with tremendous control of emotion any change at all that isn't completely conservative.

The day will come when there will be an extra infielder in exceptional cases where pitchers come to bat under compulsion from the manager to bunt. Most pitchers can't successfully bunt against such a shift even if they are good and, of course, half of the pitchers can't bunt anyway.

The thrill of a catch in the outfield: Mickey Mantle running 50 yards and making the out sitting; Al Kaline at the fence as the boys watch, Willie Mays' basket catch and Duke Snider on a "Texas leaguer." All complement the dynamic infielders.

Fielding and Defense

The purpose of team defense is to keep the opposing club from scoring runs. To many fans, fielding means simply all handling of the ball. If we accept that meaning, then pitching cannot be considered a major part of effective defense.

Pennants have been won on superior defensive ability, but good fielding without good pitching has seldom, if ever, won a pennant. The making of plays, speed afoot, strong and accurate arms, good hands, freedom from errors —all these, coupled with great effort, are of course strong contributors to a winning club. But all of them become comparatively insignificant factors if the opposing club cannot make any runs off your pitchers. An outstanding illustration of this is very real in my memory. It was in 1906, my first year in the American League. The Chicago White Sox won the American League pennant and defeated the Cubs in the World Series. That team had the lowest batting average in its league and made less runs for the season than any other club in the American League. The club was made up of puny hitters, average running speed, average throwing arms— in both outfield and infield, including catcher Sullivan. Pitchers Ed Walsh, Nick Altrock, Frank Smith, and Doc White, almost by themselves, won the pennant.

This reflection is not meant to indicate that fielding is unimportant. It is important, and a bad-fielding club has a tremendous handicap. Consider for a moment the results of technical faults in field play.

A pitcher who cannot hold runners on base allows stolen bases, which are usually improperly attributed by many fans—and some official scorekeepers—to bad catching. He is a poor defender. But worse still is the pitcher who carries his body extremely to the right or left in following through on the pitch. The ball hit through the box or behind him becomes a base hit.

The non-fielding pitcher is correctable. There is a simple rule but a difficult one for pitchers to conform to: *Move or raise the stepping foot a second time*. If the pitcher balances his weight instantly upon delivery of his pitch, he becomes an infielder able to go to his right or his left on bunts and to accommodate himself on the hard-driven ball back through the box. There is really no excuse for a major-league pitcher not to field his position. He simply needs to balance his weight on the instant following delivery.

A first baseman who takes the throw from his catcher and turns to his left to tag the runner seldom gets anybody. His body should be in position to take the throw from the catcher so that the velocity of the ball carries itself directly into the tag. This is not generally the habitual play even by major-league first basemen.

A second baseman who unbalances his body by shifting his weight right or left on the call of the pitching signal becomes dumb in trying to be smart. I know a great second baseman, now in the Hall of Fame, who had an early habit of shifting his position, several feet on occasion, according to the call of the curve or the fast ball.

A shortstop who may never have learned to hold runners on second base puts a run across the plate on a sharp single. An infielder who tags six feet above the ground instead of on the ground is a faulty fielder.

A third baseman who plays the line or shortly back of it on a dead-left-field power hitter even when the call is two strikes reminds me of the picture of one hundred years ago when the New York Knickerbocker second baseman played all the time with his foot on the second-base bag or thereabouts. The time will surely come when third basemen will play as far away from first base as the shortstop, but major-league baseball has not developed to this tactical point.

An outfielder who takes a double step after catching a fly ball seldom throws out anybody, even though he may have the reputation of a marvelous arm and good trajectory.

The photographs on these pages picture the all-out effort of the infielders and outfielders in fielding and play making to cut down the enemy on the bases. The fan, I have always felt, enjoys watching the game more if he is aware of the correct technique involved on the diamond. There is satisfaction when the second baseman takes the throw from left field, turns and tags the sliding runner after he has hit what might have been a double. But how did the runner round first, how well did he slide and in which direction? How did the second baseman place his feet to take the throw, how did he make the tag? How did the outfielder play the ball off the wall, pick it up and throw?

Because the individual techniques involved in one such base hit are relatively simple and seem the same as those in other baseball plays, the fan tends to disregard them and only watches for the umpire's safe or out sign. There is not enough enjoyment in this, it seems to me, even if your team wins. The awareness of the artfulness of every play on the field is what makes baseball exciting. As you see the runner's footwork at first and his cut to second, you know he will make it. If you see the outfielder reach for the ball as it comes off the wall and field it in a bad position for his throw you know he played the ball poorly. If the runner and outfielder perform perfectly, then the outcome of the play depends on the way the second baseman takes the throw. If he does it perfectly, then the tag can be averted only by a remarkable fallaway slide.

Many will tell you baseball is a slow game, but for a fan to trigger mentally a series of sharp observations building to the climax of one play such as this one requires keen insight and knowledge, for all these things happen with amazing speed. *Seeing them happen* is what makes baseball exciting and gives it speed. The fan who has no understanding naturally looks for nothing, sees little and complains the game is dull.

The Great Play

Who can really define a *great* play among professionals? Is that point that marks greatness somewhere beyond infinity? Or is greatness in the field a relative thing compared to what the other players can do? I think it is the supreme effort on a play where the out is made or a score averted on a ball that is on the razor edge of the line of possibility. It is a combination of reflex, chance, speed, control, brains, and sheer ability that succeeds when there is only *one way to make the play*. Over the years, sometimes when you see such a play you cannot believe it. But you *know* it is great and you never forget it.

Many of DiMaggio's runs to the far stretches of the outfield and his brother Dominic's too; Billy Cox stabbing at a fierce liner at third; Phil Rizzuto "picking cherries," as Ty Cobb called it,

behind second; or George Sisler's play that I described in "The Immortals"; Duke Snider climbing the wall in Philadelphia; or Willie Mays' catch on the ball Vic Wertz hit in the 1954 series, probably the most widely publicized baseball action sequence of all time; or Willie's running catch on Furillo's drive and his reverse *leap* in the air to throw to Westrum to double Cox at the plate that nobody photographed; Jackie Robinson's play on the ground ball against the Phillies in that final game in 1951. Masterful fielding! The great play shown here is Robert Riger's complete sequence. It's 1961— the first game of the Yankee-Reds World Series —the eighth inning—a pinch hitter—a base hit becomes an out by *two full steps* on a great stop by Cletis Boyer at third base for New York.

1. Triggered by the hit, Boyer dives to hole

2. Landing hard, he traps ball with glove

3. Recovering quickly, he pushes to his knees

4. He sights first as he picks out ball

5. The stunned umpire and crowd just begin to gasp as Clete cocks arm and lifts left knee

6. Effort shows as he steps forward on left knee

7. Boyer throws ball and rocks as if standing

8. First baseman Skowron reaches for easy putout

9. Boyer tips hat to standing ovation in stadium

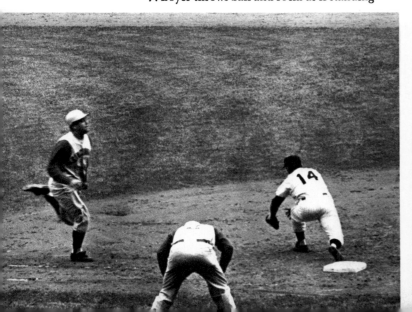

Base Running

Ty Cobb once beat me in a low-score game in Detroit in the eleventh inning—it must have been about 1915. The score was a tie in the last half of the eleventh inning when my St. Louis Browns took the field and Carl Weilman, a tall—very tall, six foot six—left-handed pitcher, with a fine record against Detroit that year, as the records will show, was pitching. As he was leaving the bench, I said to Carl, "Do you know who the third hitter is in this inning?"

He looked about and said, "Cobb."

"That's right," I said. "Don't walk him, make him hit."

Well, Carl retired the first two batsmen and Cobb came up and immediately Carl gave him four pitched balls and walked him.

Cobb immediately began prancing about off first daringly and Weilman threw over to catch him off. It was a very close play but the umpire paid no attention to it. Of course he meant that Cobb was safe. Jack Leary, the first baseman, then pretended to throw the ball back, but held it, and finally threw it back "andy over," as we used to say in the country schoolhouse—a high throw in order to tease Cobb. Cobb shot way out and quickly came back when Weilman returned the ball to Leary. There was no question in my mind that Cobb was out, but the umpire called him safe.

I called out to Jack, "Do it again, do it again." I thought it was easier and safer to get Cobb going backward than forward. Well, I wish I had never given that advice. Jack followed it, and after two or three fake moves, he threw the ball back even higher to Weilman. Cobb shot out again toward second, but he never came back. Weilman saw Cobb running, and reaching high for the ball, he dropped it in the grass at his feet and picked it up quickly and motioned toward second, having Cobb at least halfway, but there was no one at second to take the throw. Derrell Pratt, the University of Alabama boy, was far off second, and John Lavan, the University of Michigan boy, who was playing shortstop, was too far away to take a normal throw from Weilman. Weilman waited and then pressed and threw the ball in front of the bag. It bounced over Lavan's hands into center.

Cobb came racing down, touched second, and never stopped. He had no chance for third but he kept on going. The ball was fielded by Clarence "Tillie" Walker—a great arm, an accurate thrower. He threw the ball down toward third base to Jim Austin, the third baseman, who went up ten feet in front of the bag to take the throw on the first bounce. He had Cobb easily, but Austin had full knowledge of the abandoned slide of this fellow Cobb, and with one eye on the ball and possibly the other on Cobb's spikes, he dropped it on the ground in front of him. He picked it up and actually waited a part of a second for the tag of Cobb. Cobb made an early slide. He had reflexes in his

heels. He didn't have time to telegraph to his brain and get back instructions to slide ten feet in front of third, but he did. He kicked the ball out of Austin's hands, and it went with some speed to the three-foot fence forty feet beyond third.

Cobb jumped up, touched third, and went on home to score the winning run in the eleventh inning on a base on balls before another ball was ever pitched to a succeeding batsman. I saw the Detroit players reaching for their sweaters on top of the dugout. I saw 18,000 people start tumbling out of the stands, and I saw the umpires start for their dressing room.

I rushed up to the umpire, Tom Connolly, joined by Austin and others, and I was calling out, "Interference, interference, Tom, he never made any effort to touch the bag," and all that sort of conversation when Mr. Tom Connolly turned to me and said, "Mr. Rickey, give the boy credit, he made his own breaks."

Because of the nonenforcement of the balk rule, base running has lost the attractive feature of base stealing, but base stealing is not the sum total of base running. Prior to the early thirties, base stealing was an art much studied and much practiced, and even before then, one player on any and all clubs stole as many bases as and

usually more than an entire club has stolen in recent years. There are some features of base running which are just as important now as formerly. Unfortunately, less drilling and instruction are given to the players at the present time than were given when a stolen base was an attractive suspense feature of practically every game.

Many major-league base runners run a distance of ninety feet in not less than one hundred feet and some as much as one hundred ten feet, apparently forgetting that a straight line is the shortest distance between two points. You will doubtless see runners in every major-league game who on singles will run into foul territory as much as twelve feet before reaching first base. It is very hard to convince some of them that they should not circle first base with the prospective or possible chance of going on to second. Even an attendance at Ty Cobb's self-imposed practice of turning first base on a right angle would not impress them. He tried his best to reduce his running distance to first to exactly ninety feet, and he practiced turning the bag many, many times, with hard impact with the left foot, if possible, turning as squarely as he could toward second. He wouldn't circle any

base. I can still see his body squirm or twist to cut out unnecessary footage into second.

There is another asset in base running that is very important: sliding. Skill in sliding is a matter of practice. Many of the base runners in the major leagues steal an imaginary base ninety-three feet from first base at the same time they touch the ninety-foot bag at second. For example, in a slide to the right, the right foot may erroneously pass the second-base bag two to five feet in advance of the touching foot. Pictures prove this statement to be absolutely true. It requires practice to change the direction and body position of the takeoff when starting the slide. Sliding is practiced very little in most spring-training camps. The sliding pits are prepared but not used. Florida sunshine gets at least several hours every day of complete disuse. Baseball is far behind the techniques of practice employed by both football and basketball. It is a sad commentary.

A winning team has to run. Frankly, I would prefer a player who will embrace a rational adventure than a field full of know-it-alls who do nothing. Willie Mays (below), when he first came to New York, had this aggressiveness on the bases.

The Intimidator

Not only can superb skill and sheer adventure on the part of a baserunner demoralize an opposing pitcher, or a whole team for that matter, but it can almost upset the rival manager. Only once in all my lifetime have I ever known a manager to bring in a pitcher for the express purpose of holding the baserunner—where the pitching to the batsman was apparently entirely secondary to holding the runner at first. This happened in the second game of the 1962 playoffs between San Francisco and Los Angeles at Chavez Ravine. With Maury Wills on first, Manager Al Dark of San Francisco called in left-hander Dick LeMay. It was the ninth inning and the score was tied 7–7. I don't know whether the pitcher had any mind of his own, but he obviously didn't have his mind on the batsman. He threw seven consecutive times to first to hold Wills, finally walked the hitter and was relieved. Wills moved on to second, and a few minutes later scored the winning run. The following afternoon *(below, right)* he stole his record 104th base!

Such is the contributing history of Cobb and Sisler, Robinson (at left) and Wills, who won so many games although their devastating effects on the opposition may not have appeared in the box scores. They scared the opposition to death. Their presence on base would shake the coolness of a Bonaparte. When *they* got on base the whole objective of the game changed for the team in the field. *That's the great effect of reputation.*

With speed and daring, Maury Wills takes big lead. He is set to get back to first, or take key cross step on break and be gone as pitcher releases ball to steal second on catcher's hurried throw.

The Fan

Now, you have to care about baseball. "Baseball *is* caring," a literary man who is an ardent baseball fan once wrote. Of course, you have to know the game—you have to be aware of all of the possible interactions on the diamond and understand all the possible play-making situations to really enjoy baseball. But most of all, you must care about the men who play the game. Particularly the great men. The Spahns and Fords and Koufaxes, the Musials and Williamses and Mayses—and you must care about *everything* they do in a game and how they do it; you must enjoy their mannerisms and gestures, their strengths and skills; *each day* of the season you must care about what they do and how they do. You must have an appetite for baseball. This is what sustains the interest—the fanaticism. This is why the fan will do anything to see a game, *even try to parachute in!*

Times have changed, and our nervous systems have changed to adjust to the increased pace and pressures, but the game of baseball has not changed. It was designed to be played just so. For many people it is hard to adjust to the pace of a ball game today. The days feel shorter than they were in 1936—some people are exposed to so many daily shocks that the impact of baseball is too gentle.

In football, if a mercurial pass catcher races into the end zone and dives for the ball and crashes against two leaping defensemen and then falls to the ground half dead, it is a thrilling sight and a great effort. The body contact is expected and anticipated. In baseball, if two outfielders collide it is absurd. That's not the way you play the game. There is no sense comparing baseball to any other game because it is not like any other game.

This is why the young boys who fall in love with baseball remain faithful and continue the romance most of their adult lives. The baseball fan is devoted to the individual player—to his virtuosity. The image of his idol is indelible. The favorite player's performance prevails above all the minor tragedies of a boy's life and the petty problems of millions of adults.

Behind Forbes Field an elderly fan perches on a rooftop, unmindful of a possible fall, but with a blanket to protect his trousers, to see Bill Mazeroski's welcome on the homer that crushed the Yankees *(below)*.

Roger Maris watches as his 60th home run sails into the right-field seats in Yankee Stadium on September 26, 1961. Below he drives his 61st on the final day and hits his 62nd to turn the Cincinnati World Series.

The Records

The box scores are in numerical form, a cold capsule of a man's and a team's performance in a single game. But added together over the years, categorized, tabled, averaged, dated, they have become the massive archive that is the mortar with which baseball is held together. They are a schoolboy's lessons.

Records are sometimes distinguished, sometimes unenviable, sometimes "unbeatable," sometimes, by sheer weight of time and circumstances, unchallengeable, like Cy Young's 511 victories as a pitcher.

They say records are made to be broken. They have become part of the incentive for effort. But who would have thought that in the three years this book was in preparation three of baseball's most incredible and "unbeatable" records would be broken—Ruth's season record of 60 home runs, his record of 29 and 2/3 consecutive scoreless innings of World Series pitching, and Ty Cobb's season record of 96 stolen bases.

Roger Maris's feat of hitting 61 home runs in 1961 (in the extended season of 162 games) was the most sensational news story in baseball history, surpassing for sheer weight of reporting and fan interest any previous baseball feat.

The announcers and the reporters are the other vital link with the public. The incomparable Red Barber *(right)* and his protégé Vince Scully *(center)*, Mel Allen, Curty Gowdy, Waite Hoyt, Russ Hodges, are members of millions of families. In the newspapers the morning after, the admired baseball writers Arthur Daley *(left)*, John Drebinger, Red Smith, Dick Young, Joe Williams, Sid Keener, Chilly Doyle, Harry Salsinger, John B. Olds, and Vincent X. Flaherty have sustained the imagery and described the fleeting moments that grow into lasting records.

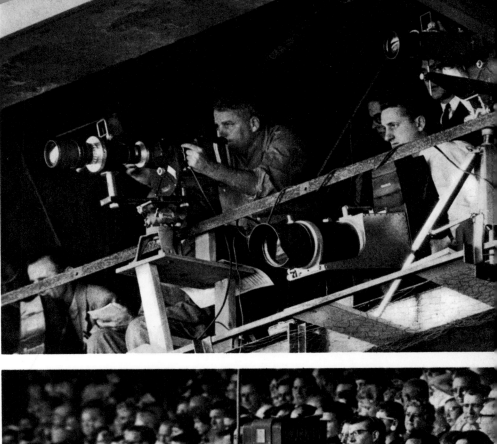

Over 35,000 baseball action pictures and portraits are taken by wire services, newspapers and magazines each year, plus the all-seeing eye of TV cameras.

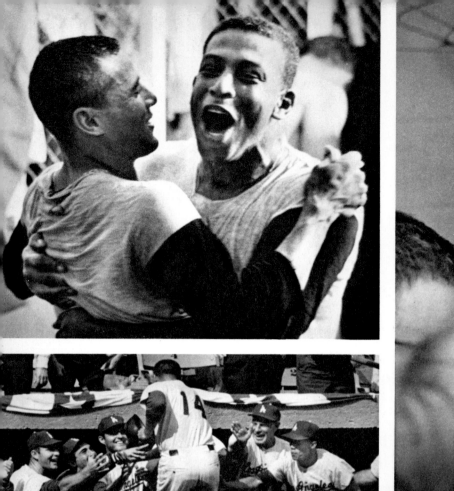

Two-hundred-pound men hugging, dancing, kissing! At left, Cepeda's roar, right, Willie's wonderful smile; the dugout welcome after a vital homer; victory banners, slogans and trinkets.

Victory Is Sweet!

There is really no way to describe the joy of victory on the diamond. As in all sports, victory is sweet. When the hardened professionals have gone through an intense game, a crucial series, a play-off or the seventh game that decides a World Championship, there is really nothing to compare with the hysteria and pandemonium that is known only in baseball.

The great moments are legend: when New York celebrated after McGraw's Giants beat Philadelphia four games to one in the first World Series where every game was a shutout; the triumph of George Stallings' miracle Braves; the Gas House Gang beating Connie Mack's great team; Gabby Hartnett's home run in Chicago and Bobby Thomson's implausible home run against Brooklyn, or Mazeroski's ninth inning hit over the fence that left the town in a delirious shambles *(top right)* and gave Pittsburgh its first Championship in 33 years; the wild antics inside a clubhouse *(left)* after the Giants beat the Dodgers in their 1962 play-off; the genuine congratulations between Fred Hutchinson *(below left)* who lost a championship, and Ralph Houk who won.

But the supreme joy is known by the young fans. While teammates hug the victorious New York pitcher Johnny Kucks *(below)* after the final game of the 1956 World Series in Ebbets Field, the young boys with their schoolbooks are first on the field (they probably got their tickets as a last-minute gift by some businessman) and in the October sunlight they enjoy a moment of victory they will never forget.

October Classic

In 1949, as president of the Brooklyn club, I was offered $150,000 for the rights to televise the Dodger games. I rejected the bid—to the dismay of our stockholders. This was an enormous amount of money in the days when baseball first appeared on television before sizable audiences. The advertising agency people showed me charts of statistics on how radio broadcasts had added to baseball attendance. Their argument was that television would do the same thing. I knew then they were wrong and I told them so.

"Radio stimulates interest. Television satisfies it," was my answer.

Time has proved me right, excepting, of course, in a World Series.

In 1963, the World Series between Los Angeles and the New York Yankees (*left*) was won in four straight games by the National League Club. It was a historic blow to the Yankee power image—a blow that may have repercussions until 1970. It was even more historic in that *over 65 million homes* were tuned in to the four-day games with the final Sunday game on NBC Television setting the largest single program viewership record in history with 27,750,000 homes watching. *This tied the Presidential Election returns of 1960 for U.S. television viewership.* The third game of the Series had twenty-five and a half million viewers.

When baseball is at its best, no sport can beat it for national interest. That was true in 1949 and is true today.

At every baseball game I attend, I dictate brief notes each inning to my secretary. I've always done this. It has given me a clear and valuable file on players and teams and, especially, it pinpoints important player abilities and frailties and documents where and when they happened and what the game situation was at the moment.

My notes for October 2, 1963, on that lovely sunny day in Yankee Stadium for the first game of the 59th World Series appear below.

October 2, 1963

As I look at these two teams in the scorecard lineup before the game, I observe that the Yankee batting order shows no weakness anywhere. There is no substitute player on the list.

As I see the Dodger lineup, the third baseman is that old pro—the pro's pro they call him—Junior Gilliam. The so-called regular is injured. Skowron, the former Yankee, is at first base. Position for position, catcher to center fielder, the Yankees on paper look solidly better. The only place for Dodger pref-

erence is in the pitching, and with the great veteran Ford pitching for the Yankees, it is almost effrontery to say that any pitcher can beat Ford. Koufax, the left-handed strikeout king of the Dodgers, can and I believe will, if necessary, pitch with two days' rest. The series could easily turn on this one pitcher.

END OF THE FIRST INNING:

Nobody on base for either club. Ford struck out two Dodgers; Koufax struck out three Yankees—Kubek, Richardson, and Tresh. This game could be a classic.

END OF THE SECOND INNING:

Frank Howard, up for the Dodgers, hit to the left center field fence—four miles—lumbered to second and then lumbered home on Skowron's single through the box. Then puny hitter Tracewski singled sharply to Mantle, and with one out and runners on first and second, Roseboro lifted a high pop fly into the dead short corner of right field for a home run. Four runs and then—

Koufax struck out Mantle and Maris—five in a row—and the sixth man, Howard, hit a pop fly ball to catcher Roseboro.

THIRD INNING:

Ford with seven hits and five runs in three innings stays in on his reputation. Will he hit for himself in the last half of the fifth? I don't believe so.

FIFTH INNING:

With two out, Elston Howard got the first hit off Koufax—a single. Two men followed with singles, filling the bases. Lopez batted for Ford and registered the eleventh strikeout shown in the memorable photograph at right. Erskine holds the record of fourteen for nine innings in series play.

SIXTH INNING:

Koufax is wild, explosively wild. Is it possible that the boy has pitched himself out? He walked both Richardson and Tresh. First time he has approached three balls. Mantle with two and two popped out to Tracewski. Then with two out, Maris popped out to Wills.

Alston showed fine self-control in this inning. Almost any manager would have had a conversation with Koufax, long ago. Koufax actually acted nervous—his pitching was a pressing performance. He tried to put more on the fast ball than he had, and only one curve during the inning seemed to be within the strike zone.

EIGHTH INNING:

Koufax shows some signs of being poohed out. He presses on every pitch, is wild. Pitching too fast. It is not that anybody is batting Koufax's brains out, not at all. The point so obvious is that

the Koufax previous to the sixth inning is not the Koufax in the eighth inning. He is now simply a good pitcher. Alston went out and evidently told him, "There are two out and Maris is the hitter. Forget striking out. Get Maris and if you are pretty tired I will relieve you in the next inning. Just get Maris and the inning is over." He did.

NINTH INNING:

Koufax is the greatest pitcher in baseball and one of the greatest of all time. He finished strong —a pinch hitter has no chance against Koufax. He is a complete bewilderment to any batsman on the first facing.

This Series is now favorable to the Dodgers. Koufax can win it—just Koufax.

Johnny Podres (*left*) won the second game in New York, 4-1. Don Drysdale (*bottom left*) over-powered the Yankees in Chavez Ravine (*below*), shutting them out 1-0. Koufax (*right*) was jubilant as his teammates carried him off the field after the 2-1 fourth game victory for the world championship—and the first sweep ever made against the Yankees in a World Series.

I thought back to that first October classic in 1905 when Mathewson pitched three shutouts... those years between just about matched my lifetime in baseball.

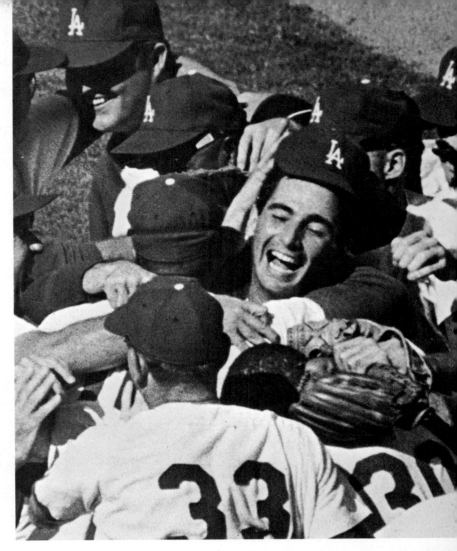

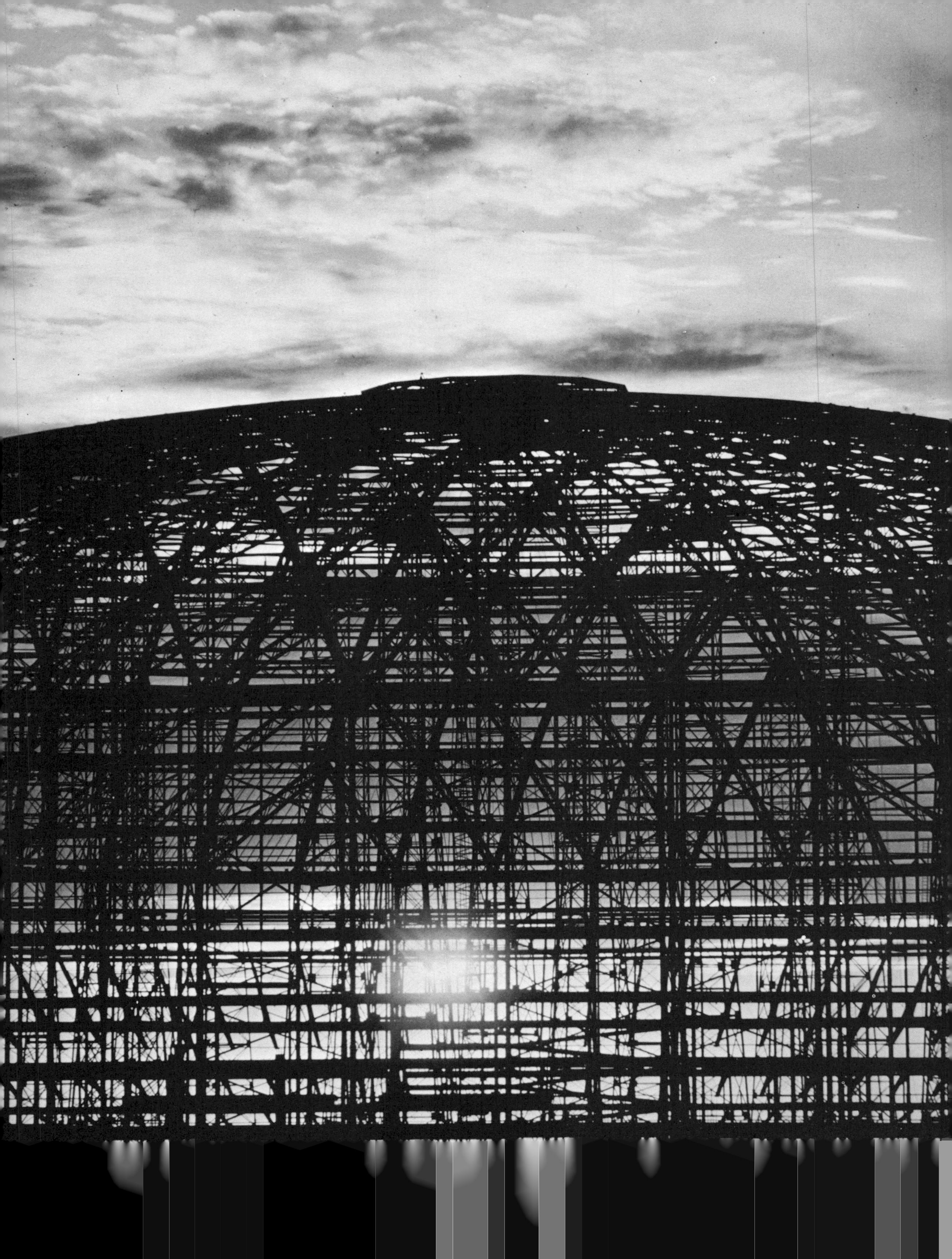

PART THREE

The Future of the Game

We have come a long way. I can remember as clearly as if it were yesterday arriving at Pennsylvania Station in New York and riding uptown in Manhattan to join the High-landers as a catcher at their ball park on 168th Street and Broadway in 1907. There is a monumental hospital on that site today. They are tearing down Penn Station as they tore down Ebbets Field and the Polo Grounds, and if John McGraw ever came back to town, he would be surprised indeed. The face of the country and the world is changing, and I wonder if baseball is ready for the future.

Baseball is building for the future! Chavez Ravine, the split-level extravaganza in Los Angeles, the strong concrete circle of Candlestick Park in San Francisco, and the William A. Shea Stadium in New York are modern and really beauti-ful structurally. And the newest marvel of them all, in Houston, Texas, appears in the revealing picture on the opposite page. We have come a long way from the low wooden fence that bordered the diamond upon Broadway in 1907, my last year as a player in professional baseball.

Now, do you know what the glamorous new domed sta-dium in Houston may turn into as time goes by? A television studio! They may conduct great sports spectaculars under the closed-in-glass architectural masterpiece and record them on video tape. You may see track meets, equestrian jumping, rodeos... all under the most favorable conditions, and indoors. Imagination may be stretched a bit to think that an occasional canned baseball doubleheader might be filmed in the blazing sunshine, and you may watch it months later on a cold, miserable night in Chicago on the late show. The ball game will be a spectacle to bridge the gap between commercials. Some people say that going out to the ball park will become fashionable only to see the World Series. I know a distinguished writer who insists that baseball parks will be transformed into television studios because they will be almost empty; that the attendance problem will be hurt-ing the game so badly that management will find it much cheaper to send all the ticket sellers, vendors and ushers home and just let the television crew in.

Football must not become our national pastime. Profes-sionally it will grow, and someday it may even command the public's allegiance as much as baseball does, but it will never replace baseball as our national game.

Why not? Because football cannot be played by young boys safely in the heat of summer when they are off from school. A mother cannot send her son out and trust him to an afternoon of football, even with the finest equipment and coaching. It is too rough a contact sport for young limbs—and if you appraise the modern safety equipment, who can afford it? Dungarees, a dollar cap and a glove will last three summers and return fifty times the initial cost to a boy who plays baseball. I like football. I played it pro-fessionally one year, coached it, watch it all the time. But baseball is the game for boys. Baseball is not in danger at all in this country but the professional game is.

Professional football has expanded its teams in recent years and has grown tremendously in public favor. Between 1948 and 1964 pro football attendance showed a phenom-enal rise of 215.2%. Professional football developed the player draft, which equalized talent throughout the league. For years the teams participated equally in the selection of new material and this is the key to pro football's success.

Professional baseball is confronted with two major prob-lems: first, equalization of teams; and second, expansion. A third problem is television and public relations, which in immediate urgency is considerably subordinate to the first two but must not be overlooked in professional baseball's future.

The First Problem: Equalizing the Teams

Close competition is the lifeblood of any sport. The inor-dinate weakness of many teams to field top players because they were unable to match the bonus bidding of wealthier clubs has hurt baseball and led to a lack of close competi-tion. In the American League the pennant race, in the minds of most of our fans, was over in March in many recent campaigns.

One of the most popular points of hot-stove discussions among the fans and repeated conversations among baseball officials over the years has always been—Why do the Yankees win? They have won for several reasons: their willingness to spend money because they had it, although they were never outstanding in awarding lavish bonuses; their na-tional prestige that created in the minds of the youth of this country one idea—that everything else being equal, a boy would like to play for the Yankees. But more than these two, the Yankees' consistent success was due to the intelligent toil of Ed Barrow and George Weiss in the front office. Miller Huggins, Joe McCarthy and Casey Stengel were highly intelligent baseball men and the best of managers, but over the years they reaped undue acclaim compared to the almost forgotten general managership that made their success possible. Barrow provided the Yankee scouting system with three or four of the best judges of free agency talent that baseball ever knew, hired them and kept them, as I have cited in my tribute to him in The Immortals.

Nevertheless, there must be an effort to equalize the opportunity of *all clubs* in the leagues in the securing of young talent. The Yankee success story is not due to the play of luck or fortune at all. It is the result of excellence primarily in the front office. But the fact remains that both the American and National Leagues are not balanced from top to bottom. The Yankee success simply has exaggerated this imbalance.

Now, the wealth of the world could be redistributed among all mankind today... and tomorrow you would have paupers and millionaires all over again. You cannot equalize the ingenuity and effort of the individual, and no one wants to. There never will be a way to equalize individual ability such as the Yankees have had. But there must be *legislation to establish equal opportunity for all clubs in the field of young talent.*

The Blue Book, baseball's compendium of information, gives the complete list of registered scouts employed by the twenty major-league clubs, showing the number of scouts to be 668. Some of these are commission scouts or "bird dogs" or part-timers. The average number of full-time scouts will be not less than fifteen per club, with an average salary of $8,000. This makes a scouting cost to each club of $120,000 per year.

The traveling and living expenses of scouts have kept pace with the advance of salaries. Most scouts will average 40,000 miles by automobile annually; at ten cents per mile the average traveling expense per scout is $4,000. Meals, lodging and entertainment will average $15 per day. Assuming that each scout will give 200 days each year to field work, this item amounts to $3,000. Fifteen scouts per club will then cost each club $105,000 for expenses. For the sake of a conservative estimate, let us reduce this figure to $80,000. The total scouting cost per club will then amount to $200,000 each year.

Major-league clubs generally assign their scouts on the basis of territorial coverage. Until recent years, it used to be that scouting was simply the finding of players. The bonus orgy changed all that. Today, finding the player is just as easy as it ever was, but the finding is now only a small part of the job. A scout of today must be a salesman. He must be able to sign the player to a contract. And, in the face of reckless competition, the scout is inclined to use the owner's money without too much consideration for the club's stockholders' dividends at the end of the year. And the bonus mounts! The fact is that a scout who has found a prospective player will spend many times more hours with the player and his parents than he takes in the finding, and the central office must usually join in the effort to secure the player. This central office force will cost every club for yearly salary and expenses in excess of $50,000 per club.

It is simple addition of the above to say that every one of the twenty major-league clubs will average on direct scout-

ing expense $120,000 for salaries, plus $80,000 for personal expenses, plus $50,000 for the central office—a sum of $250,000 *before* they have paid a single bonus. Twenty clubs, therefore, spend each year a net sum of $5,000,000 for scouting, and at that point, not a penny yet for bonuses.

Now let us see what pooled scouting will cost each club.

An exhaustive questionnaire will be sent to each of the 668 registered scouts in the Blue Book. In addition all professional clubs, both major and minor, would be asked to submit recommendations of worthwhile scouts. Then the pooled scouting department as set up by the major leagues would contract for not more than fifty scouts instead of the 300 now employed by the twenty teams, who would cover the entire field of both professional and amateur baseball, including the colleges and high schools. With salaries on an average of $10,000 per man we now have an initial salary expenditure for scouting of $500,000. Living expenses and transportation can safely be placed at $5,000 per scout or $250,000.

Each scout will cover several times the area now covered because his job is simply to find players—not to stay with them and baby them half the season in order to sign them up. These fifty men will be the best in the whole field of baseball scouting. Whereas each of the twenty clubs at present frequently acts initially upon the report of only one scout, *each major-league club under the proposed plan would be able to get the most expert information from no less than three high-class scouts on practically every prospective player.* Scout information, in writing, would be photocopied daily and sent to the president of every professional club, both major and minor. Each club would get more dependable information covering the field of ability, availability, and probability from the fifty nonpartisan institutionalized scouts than they are now receiving from the present fifteen per club, one man to a spot, covering the entire country.

Good ballplayers will consistently be found more quickly. Every boy in America who wanted to play professional baseball would want to get on that accredited list—and all would be putting out in every game. They might not even know they had made the list because they would not be approached or solicited at all. The possibility of a hidden prospect would be remote.

The central player-production agency would cost administratively not more than $200,000 a year plus a generous $50,000 for rent, insurance, travel, salary and incidentals. These figures add up to an exact total of $1,000,000—*which covers the complete production of players annually from the free-agency field.*

Now let us examine the total cost of free-agency scouting under the present bonus practice. One of our National League organizations produced in less than two years more than one hundred free-agent players. Another major-league organization, including its five farm clubs, produced between sixty and seventy. It is my experience that any enterprising major organization scouting staff should produce assuredly more than forty free agents for its organizational trial—some without any bonus whatever. For the sake of safety, let us say that the average production number of signed players per major-league organization is forty. Most of the forty will receive a bonus of some amount, some in the high figures, some nominal. Player Robert Bailey, reportedly receiving a $180,000 bonus from Pittsburgh, is an exception, but several players receive a bonus of more than $50,000.

Sixteen players in 1964 received more than $30,000 each. In order to be ultra-safe in our estimate, let us put the average bonus price at a paltry $7,500. Forty times $7,500 makes a total average bonus payment per organization of $300,000 annually. Twenty major-league organizations will then spend $6,000,000 per year for bonuses plus $5,000,000 for scouting expenses. The major-league presidents' reports and the report of the National Association of Professional Baseball Clubs, I believe, will show these estimates to be accurate.

Therefore the total cost of free-agency production per year amounts to $11,000,000.

In other words, baseball can reconstruct its free-agency production with more exhaustive and more dependable information at a cost of $1,000,000 instead of the $11,000,000 they are now spending. These figures on our present production costs are not unreasonable and the estimates on the substitute budget are completely liberal. This means a saving to baseball of $10,000,000 per year, or $500,000 for each club. An incredible saving!

Now some questions arise, and the first one is, "Where are you going to get the $1,000,000 to cover this pooled-scouting expense? Well, first of all, the major-league clubs could, should and would put it up. And if some club insists that the two major leagues do not spend $11,000,000 over-all on recruiting, let such a club name the total figure. Anything over $1,000,000 is economically unsound. Let us look at the sureness of pooled scouting.

For this reason alone, the second most important challenge to professional baseball is expansion!

It is to the accomplishment of these two ends—equalization and expansion—that I carefully explain my ideas on the future of the game.

The first problem in equalization is the bonus.

Ownership must eliminate the bonus. The club owners of the two major leagues could elect, I am sure, a commissioner who would enforce a bonus rule. Personal favor, prestige of name, politics in a sense, and actual aggressive belief by a few owners in no bonus rule at all—each and possibly all may influence the selection of the next commissioner. It is not probable that the next commissioner will be elected on the basis of a commitment to enforce a bonus rule. As a matter of fact, that commitment would be the greatest single qualification of a new commissioner—for the sake of economy to the owners, fairness to the players, and equality of playing strength of competing teams. With this high improbability in mind, I offer a different solution to the bonus problem, and I will call it "pooled scouting."

But first let me examine the iniquitous character of the bonus. The bonus is bad from start to finish, and for the following reasons:

1. It is bad for the boy, say an eighteen-year-old youth, to come into possession of unheard-of sums of money, unearned to begin with, and probably ill-spent to end with. A new car, an impulsive marriage, or the very frequent capitalizing of a father's foolish adventure into a strange business—these and many other avenues of inexperienced investment lose their importance when we consider the moral wreck frequently resulting from the ill-advised use of money by these teenage players.

2. Player salaries should be related to attendance and income at the gate. Club owners, under the present bonus, are practically compelled to pay all established players whatever they ask after they are reminded that an untried, inexperienced youngster has received a fabulous amount of money to sign his contract. Consequently, salaries are double what they should be on the basis of *the club's income at the gate*. On this basis only, most clubs lose money.

3. The bonus has not only unfairly affected salaries, it can be and frequently is an effective disturber of team morale—off the field, in the clubhouse, and even *on* the field. The injustice and unfairness of bonuses to kids affect the thinking of the player roster as a whole.

4. Inexperience, tender age, unknown disposition, poor health, lack of skills, no records, the amazing prevalence of early arm injury, and above all, the statistical fact that the great majority of bonus players do not have major league physical ability, make the bonus investment the most hazardous expenditure of money that I can think of.

To illustrate how ludicrous the bonus is, suppose a senior in a local high school in St. Louis, who writes well compared to his colleagues on other high school papers, is the editor-in-chief. Now suppose further that the *Globe-Democrat* and the *Post-Dispatch* in St. Louis undertake to sign the boy to a contract as a sports writer—a reporter, indeed. Competition gets tough and the *Post-Dispatch* finally signs him with a bonus of $50,000 plus a good salary. There is more sense on the part of the two newspapers to embrace that asinine risk than there is for twenty clubs to compete in the signing of the local high school pitcher. The writer does not have the same hazard of incapacitation because of physical injury, nor of team acceptance and adjustment. There is higher mortality among young baseball players than there is among young journalists.

5. The fear of losing a possibly great player, with the wild bidding that always follows, causes extravagant bonuses which violate all basic realism in economic history. Something for nothing may be an objective among many slothful, unthrifty segments of our people, who seem to believe that the world or the nation or the community owes them a living; but it has no place in baseball because it tends to damn the player, wreck the club and bankrupt the owner.

6. Most important of all, the bonus is unfair to every club that cannot compete in financial bidding contests. Money-poor clubs cannot enter the market. It should be the objective in all sports, including professional baseball, that money should not be the most powerful factor in determining the winning ability of a team. Any rule that makes sweat and toil and good judgment the controlling items in making and maintaining strength is a good rule. And any rule that minimizes these factors and makes money dominant is a bad rule. To the extent that baseball removes money from the picture, it makes the game fair and challenging. "By the sweat of thy face shall a club earn a pennant" should not be said as a penalty but rather as a benediction. Every club should have a fair chance at a young player, regardless of money.

My purpose in pointing out the objections to the bonus is to show that it is completely absurd, especially when you consider that *nine out of ten bonus players who are paid $8,000 or more fail to make good in the majors!* If any other business in this country were to practice a bonus rule as baseball does, it would reap only shame and ridicule.

My plan for the future of the game, pooled scouting, will help solve the mechanical imbalance of the leagues and more economically equalize the playing strength of teams.

Before presenting a blueprint for pooled scouting's implementation, one must first understand the established scouting procedure.

201

These fifty high-class, industrious scouts, working under skilled direction, will produce, say, on first observation 1,000 names per year. The subsequent scouting will probably reduce the figure to 500, and the final scouting recommendation will reduce the figure to half that. And now this final list is ready for all of baseball to examine from copious records. The draft from this list will proceed on exactly the same basis as the present draft, which in itself is to be interfered with in no way.

Two draft dates per year would be established, one approximately June 15, the other approximately December 15. The teams would draft in exactly the same order as in the existing draft. The price of each player could be $10,000, or such price as the major leagues agreed upon, and each club would be privileged to draft until it reached its player limit. Following the major-league draft would be the AAA and so on down the line. Instead of signing forty free-agent players as we have indicated as the average for each organization, let us say that each organization would take only ten players on an average, an expenditure of $100,000 per club. Twenty clubs would then pay $2,000,000 into the scouting department treasury, an amount exactly double the entire pooled scouting cost. At $5,000 per draft and only ten players per club, the scouting expense of $1,000,000 is met.

If more than 200 were drafted at $10,000 each, there would be additional profit of $10,000 per draft, in addition to the first million. Now, it is reasonable to believe that an additional five drafts per club would be made, thus adding another million to the profits. If organized baseball were to give the exclusive marketing rights of all free-agent players to an independent corporation, such a corporation would gladly pay $1,000,000 annually, in advance, for such rights.

Of course, the major leagues should not farm out this program. It should be an integral part of their own business. They would not be robbing themselves of the first $1,000,000 spent. They would simply be getting that amount back from the draft and at the same time adding an extra $2,000,000 to the scouting treasury. This answers the question of financing pooled scouting.

It is obviously possible that fuller information on more players will result from pooled scouting, in which case each of twenty major-league clubs, together with their farm clubs, would like to draft more than the player limit now permits. If so, they could very easily raise the player limit to 45 or 50—a matter for them to decide. Likewise, the major leagues could raise their option list to 18 or 20. It further seems reasonable to assume that ownership would keep unrestricted control of a drafted player's contract for a period of three calendar years following the draft.

Another question may be, What about the hidden player, meaning a player not previously reported by the scouting commission? What of the possibility that this or that club might know of a player not included in the recommended list? A period of thirty days immediately following the draft dates should be provided during which time every club could negotiate without restriction with any player anywhere. At the expiration of the thirty days, the exclusion period would again apply. Thus the freedom of contract would be enhanced. The "restraint of trade" item which might be raised would be considerably answered. I do not believe that there would be any signing during this period other than a new boy who might come to attention suddenly because of a late showing or recovery from an injury during that thirty-day period.

The bidding competition under the pooled scouting program I am now proposing for the future *removes all competitive bidding*, except for the two unrestricted one-month periods each year, and allows the weaker teams to build up their strength through the draft without financial handicap.

The question of what the draft price should be for the AAA clubs can be decided easily by a conference between the majors and the minors. It occurs to me that the higher minors and particularly the majors would recognize the benefit that might accrue to the independently owned AAA, AA and A leagues if they were permitted to select from the leftovers as many players as their player limit allowed at no draft price whatever. These lower clubs that are owned or controlled by the major-league clubs would pay the regular draft price with possibly agreed protection for three years. Thus there would be all kinds of incentive for the extension of professional baseball in the minors.

From the standpoint of the public and of most of the owners, this program of pooled scouting would permit equal distribution of talent each year and thereby have a strong tendency to equalize the playing strength of clubs. The ultimate ideal of the program would be that every club become the equal of every other club. That there would be no so-called ignominious tail-enders or 100-game losers, year in and year out. Even the new clubs in the present illogical ten-club league could conceivably win half their games within two years. This equitable distribution of players, tending to create a pennant chance for every club, would intensify public interest, resulting in more money at the gate.

The construction of my pooled scouting plan was completed in 1963 and was outlined in conversation to many of my friends in the major leagues. In 1965 four clubs, Milwaukee, Pittsburgh, Cleveland, and Detroit got together and began a collective scouting plan which undoubtedly will furnish increased information on players, and financial savings to each club. The idea of pooled scouting, however, cannot work unless all clubs are included, because teams not involved will have a free hand and nothing will be done toward equalization and elimination of the bonus. Only a total change in the scouting program, with all clubs included, can make pooled scouting succeed.

The Second Problem: Expansion

The second gripping challenge to the major leagues involves their expansion to include other great cities throughout our country.

The changes in postwar America in transportation and communications plus the population explosion directed the shift of baseball franchises which has somewhat nationalized the game. Unfortunately, the motivation behind these moves was not one of nationalization but of prospective profits at the gate. The abiding, cultivated sentiment of the people was disturbed. The invitation to expand came gladly from new cities and inducements were generous. Further expansion likewise would be welcomed. The needs of 190 million people for entertainment and recreation are more demanding today than they were for 76 million when the American League was founded 65 years ago.

In 1964 there were 20,000,000 boys from ages nine to eighteen playing baseball on organized sandlot or school teams in the United States. If the American League sixty-five years ago, when our country's population was 76,000,000, could endure strenuous opposition (mostly based on the alleged dearth of players) and if two years later the American League could beat the National League in a World Series, it is unthinkable to me that with a 190,000,000 population now and with the present vast expansion in amateur play, we do not have enough players to form more major leagues on the professional level.

There is, however, a plentiful supply of fine players throughout this country. The canard that there are not enough players is about played out. It is as old as the American League. Mr. Bancroft Johnson, first President of the American League, gave the answer to this 65-year-old, news-stirring, tittle-tattle when he said that there were "not enough players for the last-place National League Club or it would not be last," and within two years his new league won in the World Series.

What business is there in America that has not changed or adjusted its structure in the last sixty years? What hidden excuse can be found to justify holding to twenty clubs?

The game of baseball in its nature is almost indigenous to our country and nothing can change it. It will remain our great national game. But the two major leagues are not indigenous. Their future is in the hands of twenty corporations, and long before the year 2000 the United States will surely see either sportsmanlike expansion of professional baseball or an end to the present two-major-league monopoly.

Even if talent were thin it would make no difference in public support, for the public bases its loyalty on comparative merit and not on a dissection of individual muscle. Indeed, goodness is relative. If the team wins, it is good. If it doesn't win, it is not good. And with equalization of teams through pooled scouting, a competitive third league is eminently feasible.

The National League as we know it was organized in 1876. The American League followed twenty-five years later. There are many cities in America not now in the major leagues that have far greater populations than the original cities of the major leagues had when they were organized. Atlanta has built a park equal to our first-division best and will be a member of the National League in 1966. Cities like Buffalo, Dallas, Fort Worth—why name them all?—are anxious to have major league representation.

At present the major leagues are made up of ten clubs each. That number is unwieldy, illogical and unsatisfactory from practically every standpoint. A study of the ninety-year history of baseball will show the unwelcome features of a twelve-club league. However, the political probability is that the major leagues will expand to twelve en route to ultimate eight-club leagues. The history of the minor leagues joins with that of the majors in proving the desirability of eight-club leagues. The smaller number accommodates travel economy, player comfort, schedule making and gate receipts. Three major leagues of eight clubs each would practically double the gate receipts from the World Series, with corresponding increased income from radio and television. There is, however, serious interest in a division of a twelve-club league into East and West sections of six clubs each. If and when expansion goes to twelve clubs, the next step would doubtless be this sectional separation.

When the time comes that the major leagues face the election of a commissioner, surely they will have in mind a man committed to the expansion of professional baseball. The obligation of leadership here should be optimistically faced and courageously undertaken by the new commissioner.

There must be a steadfast motivation on the part of everyone to see to it that professional baseball expands to meet the needs of all our people and become truly national. The owners' own ultimate future depends upon it. Otherwise, some other professional sport may become dominant because of its extensive nationalization and seasonal encroachment.

How, then, can this expansion of professional baseball be accomplished? What should be the first step?

The answer is simple: A positive proposal by the commissioner for immediate expansion.

Committees appointed by the two major leagues agreed on August 6, 1959, to accept into major-league baseball eight designated cities and eight designated owners—two immediately, meaning within two years, and two within four years—in each league. The National League supported its committee on the first two, and I believe is ready to finish the job if properly approached. Whatever either league does, the other must necessarily follow.

There should be no validation of the reserve clause in baseball contracts by Congressional legislation that in itself does not protect possible expansion by including many cities as potential members of an additional major league.

Both leagues favor expansion, conversationally, but no one has proposed any move in that direction. Therefore the commissioner must be the one to act.

The commissioner could produce within a reasonable time, meaning a few weeks, four cities with ample and interested population and owners with financial strength and personal integrity. It would be impossible to keep out of public print the enterprise of his effort and its results. Therefore, he would have help from unexpected sources. If four great cities, for example, were to place their qualifications before baseball, it would be difficult to refuse them and flout public opinion. Major league owners must keep in mind that the entire public is the beneficiary of any plan for expansion. There are millions of people in the unseen audience at every negotiating conference of the two major leagues. This is doubly true because the two majors must keep in mind that the absorption of the Continental League, or its demise if you wish, was based upon the promise of the committees of the two leagues that the settlement would embrace their further expansion. Concrete proposals from four cities with every requisite qualification in full view, presented by the commissioner himself, would have wide press and public support, and the commissioner's leadership would become immediately formidable, and, I believe, followed.

No treatise on the future of professional baseball can properly disregard the recent growth of professional football. Expansion in baseball may be affected by it and at the same time be the answer to it.

It has become recognizably true that baseball suffers in attendance when the schedule clashes with football, and this disparity at the gate makes it advisable to avoid, if possible, schedule conflicts with football, either college or professional. A pro football exhibition double-header in Cleveland in August 1963 drew 75,000 and in 1964 drew 88,000 people, with gate receipts amounting to $500,000 for this one day. Double-headers will spread to other cities.

The immediate danger to baseball, however, is not so much in the comparative gate attendance of football as in the extension of the pro football season. I remember very well a joint meeting of the American and National Leagues years ago in which a National League club was severely criticized by everyone for permitting a professional football game to be played in its park a day or two prior to the close of the National League baseball season. There may soon be more and more professional football games in practically every major-league city after August 1. Is it possible that we may here and there have ownership in baseball with sufficiently lucrative business interests outside the game that make it easy to be unmindful of or indifferent to the seasonal invasion of this competing sport? *Do the baseball owners realize the decline in national baseball fan allegiance?*

The challenge to expand the major leagues is further emphasized when owners come to realize that the possible closing of the minor leagues will result in a marked decline of national interest in professional baseball.

The Third Problem: Television and Public Relations

The third problem for the future of baseball is in television. I have had long discussions with many people about this final aspect. Most everyone knows that television made football. It made it possible for millions of fans every Sunday to see a game clearly that they had never seen before. The tight formation of the offensive and defensive lines fit the shape of the television screen as if the screen had been designed for the game.

Baseball does not fit the television screen. Not yet! Consequently, the televising of baseball games has become so fragmented that the entire image of the game has been changed and reduced to a "still picture" or a series of still pictures, e.g., of pitcher and batter. The whole geometry of the diamond is considerably lost on television. The entire space relationship of infield and outfield is not seen in its full scope or is switched to so infrequently and abruptly as to impair a viewer's orientation very seriously. When the picture jumps from a tight close-up to a long shot, the impact is lost. The television of baseball is so poor that the piece of the game you are continually forced to watch is somewhat repetitive. Of course, if a man is pitching a no-hitter in the ninth inning, it is now watched on television with concentrated interest—even if they showed it through a keyhole. But I speak of the televising of the whole game over a full season.

The shape of the home television screen must be changed in the years to come. The "sports screen" doubtless will be produced by major television manufacturers on a 2 or 2½ to 1 ratio. When the width of the screen is 2½ times the height (in home projection), *then* you will see the baseball diamond in its full dimension and the interaction of its players, and when the full, wide screen is used to show a slide at second or to convey the distance an outfielder has to run to make a superb catch, the viewing will be truly exciting. The sports screen will likely take a few years, electronically—but it will come, and when it does, the televising of baseball will be the greatest beneficiary. This sports screen will also change the way baseball is reported and will give the announcers—especially those who are former players—much greater opportunity to explore the situation on the field.

Public Relations

The final point of public relations is not at all disregarded in professional baseball. It is expensively attended to in the office of the commissioner, as well as in the offices of both major leagues, and indeed, in the office of every major league club. What professional baseball needs in the field of public relations is the most imaginative, creative minds that money can buy. The devoted attention of several old-fashioned public relations departments in the game today should be revitalized by the addition of Madison Avenue's progressive public relations techniques working behind the scenes to improve baseball's image.

The public relations between baseball players and fans, particularly youngsters, are not perfect. Today some major league players, a sizable minority, are difficult to approach. Those comparative few sign nothing without a lawyer or an agent at their side, and will only reluctantly pose for newspaper photographers—let alone kids. Some players will not appear on radio or television except on "flesh and blood" terms. "A little leaven leaveneth the whole," and these few create the impression that all players are like that. Most intelligent players know that their professional careers depend upon public approval and support. It can be said without any mental reservations whatever that the professional baseball players in America are by and large gentlemen of high order, who know full well that their deportment and habits and appearance and public relations are far from trivial—either economically or culturally.

In a profession where the physical is dominant in the triune nature of man, it would be surprising indeed if we did not find here and there an occasional scalawag. I think Americans can take a justifiable pride in the character of their professional baseball players. Certainly some hazard is created when the dollar mark is placed on their muscles. Baseball is a game of great honesty, beginning with the player, then the owner, and ending with the public.

There is, naturally, criticism from some academic sources that indulgence in sports in our country is overdone. The emphasis on physical excellence in Greece, in Great Britain, and now in America does not lend support to those critical views. The remarkable essay of William James, "The Moral Equivalent of War," almost finds a philosophical place for organized sports in any society. I do not give credence to the views of those who decry the relationship between our people and their play afield. The sports writers of America, the handmaidens of the game, insure the integrity of all competitive sports for a long future. So long as baseball has commissioners such as Landis, who set the stage for it, and Chandler and Frick, who jealously guarded against even evil acquaintanceship as they have done for the last forty-five years, scandal on the playing field or off it is very remote.

All business ventures have problems, but when business is combined with sport, the problem becomes different and challenging, particularly if sport is to remain dominant over business. The hope for the successful solution of every problem facing professional baseball is based upon the integrity and devotion of the owners of the twenty major-league clubs. Without exception, the major-league clubs are owned by men of high character who are worthy of the full confidence of the public. But very few of them give full-time, personal attention to their baseball investment, and most are absentee owners. When the time comes for the owners to personally confront the problems of the game, they will deal with them directly and effectively and without unnecessary delay.

Baseball is faced with a truly history-making chance right now to give evidence of distinctive sportsmanship by making the necessary changes for the future of the game, thus making it in reality our national pastime.